NATIONAL LAMPOON®

— PRESENTS —

TRUE FACTS:
THE
BIG BOOK

The Complete, Unexpurgated Assembly of
Amazing Ads, Stupefying Signs, Weird
Wedding Announcements, and Other Absurd-
but-True Samples of Real-Life Funny Stuff

— COMPILED BY —

JOHN BENDEL & JASON WARD

CB

CONTEMPORARY BOOKS

Library of Congress Cataloging-in-Publication Data

National lampoon presents true facts : the big book / compiled by John
    Bendel & Jason Ward.
            p.   cm.
        ISBN 0-8092-3559-5 (alk. paper)
        1. American wit and humor, Pictorial.   1. National lampoon.
    I. Bendel, John.   II. Ward, Jason.   III. National lampoon.
    NC1428.N37   1995a
    031.02—dc20
                                            95-23509
                                            CIP

Portions of the material in this book were published previously in
*National Lampoon Presents True Facts: The Book, National Lampoon
Presents More True Facts, and National Lampoon Totally True Facts.*

The "Report from the Editor" has been compiled from the previous
writings of John Bendel.

20   19   18   17   16   15   14   13   12   11   10   9   8   7   6   5   4

Photo contributed by Bruce Markoe

Contents

Report from the Editor

Welcome to *National Lampoon Presents True Facts: The Big Book*, our all-star collector's volume of stories, headlines, signs, ads, photos, business cards, and, well, you name it, submitted by the readers of *National Lampoon* to a long-standing feature we call "True Facts."

What is a True Fact? It is a grain of absurd glory for the man or woman who clipped it from a newspaper, tore it from a magazine, took a picture of it, carved it on a tree, etched it in stone, wrote it in the sand, shouted it to the heavens, or whistled it on the wind. In other words, it's an odd, often ironic, yet always genuine example of real-life funny stuff. Most True Facts are unintentionally funny, but, yes, a few are obviously premeditated gags. That's because we're not trying to preserve some kind of conceptual purity here. We're just trying to have a good time.

You may be wondering, isn't every fact a True Fact? Do you mean to say there are any other kinds of facts?

But of course, faithful reader. There are sordid facts, secondhand facts, unvarnished facts, salient facts, the facts of life, just the facts . . . in fact, there are more facts than any of us might ever have imagined. Hence, it is critical to distinguish between True Facts and other, more prevalent, less intriguing, and yes, quite frankly, inferior facts. The following quiz should illuminate the essential differences.

Q. Which is the True Fact?
  A. According to the *Information Please Almanac*, Sir H. Campbell-Bannerman served as the prime minister of Britain from 1905 to 1908.
  B. According to the *Gannett Reporter Dispatcher*, a White Plains, New York, youth was charged with indecent exposure after he allegedly dropped his pants in front of a person dressed as Gumby.

Q. Which is the True Fact?
  A. A headline from a recent edition of the *New York Times* proclaimed "Dollar Off Again Against the Yen."
  B. A headline from the *Fitchburg Sentinel and Enterprise* proclaimed "Colon Outburst Highlights Trial."

In both examples, item B was, in fact, the True Fact. We're sure you'll agree with us that each outclassed its mundane competitor, clearly demonstrating the superiority of True Facts over lesser sorts of data.

Please note that the above quiz was meant for *educational purposes only*. Official True Fact classification should always be left to highly trained specialists. That would be us.

Which brings us to the point: If you have an item you believe might be a True Fact—whether it's something you've clipped or copied or photographed—please send that potential True Fact for analysis to:

True Facts
National Lampoon
10850 Wilshire Boulevard
Suite 1000
Los Angeles, CA 90024

(That's what Jeff Reed, who submitted the Gumby True Fact, and Bruce Siart, who submitted the Colon True Fact, did—and *now their names are in print*.)

Experts will subject your submission to technical evaluation under highly controlled conditions and come to a determination. If tests prove positive, *your name* will accompany your True Fact upon publication, forever placing you in the bright and shining light of True Facts glory.

By the way, because of the volume of mail, we disregard all submissions on rock, wood, wind, or the wings of angels.

Thank you.

You may read the rest of the book now.

Signs of Life

Photo contributed by Ted Goldsmith

Put a gorgeous dame on my chest, and make 'er a spaniel.

JAE-MAR-S M 86
ACADEMY OF DOG OBEDIENCE / ALL B
DOG TATOOING!
JULY 15 & 18

Photo contributed by Andy Altschuler

Photo contributed by Jack Dakin

. . . and the service will start as soon as He comes out.

Photo contributed by Mike Sellers

Jet-Propelled?

Photo contributed by Terry Hollis

She can hardly wait.

Photo contributed by
Virgil Rossner

Photo contributed by
Michael Landau

Photo contributed by Nicole Parsons

4

Picnic Hell

Photo contributed by Brian Weaver

Photo contributed by Chris Kidd

Name That Hole

Photo contributed by D. J. Hartley

Photo contributed by David Ferrall

Photo contributed by Pete Markay

Little Enigmas, Part I

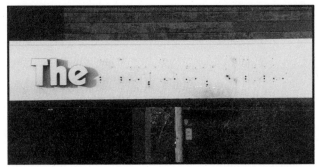

Photo contributed by J. Brown

Photo contributed by Mark Pauga

Actually, the dogs aren't all that bad.

Photo contributed by Karen Lee

Well, not all *that* new.

Photo contributed by
Theodore S. Bowes

A politician by any other name . . .

Photo contributed by Rob Culbertson

Zoogz Knows His People

Photo contributed by George Smith

The New Math

The Gramercy Arts Trio
Beautiful music for memorable moments
Weddings • Receptions • Parties
Flute • Violin • Cello & Vocalist

Ad from *New Jersey Monthly* magazine;
contributed by Al Evans

Dine With

Chris Demo Gus George
THREE BROTHERS RESTAURANT

Business card contributed by Ralph Gates

Quick! Into the shelter! Here come the customers!

Photo contributed by Corey Anderson

It's right next door to Big Al's 24-Hour Cathedral.

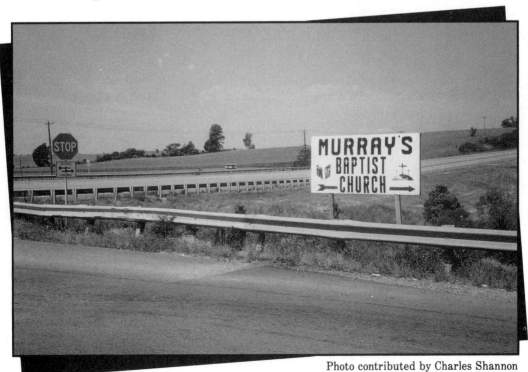

Photo contributed by Charles Shannon

Dream Boats

Photo contributed by Jim McLaughlin

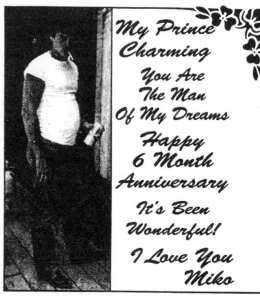

Ad from the San Luis Obispo County, California,
Telegram-Tribune; contributed by Paul Velardi

Fast Food

Photo contributed by Steve Bouchard

Peach pits, apple cores, and banana peels to your left.

Photo contributed by Karen Lee

And the kids don't look so swell either.

Photo contributed by Chris Gutscher

11

Kids Over the Hill

ADULT CHILDREN

Photo contributed by Denis Navarro

Old Children's Books 734 →

Photo contributed by Oswald F. Angst

HOME COOKED FOOD
EVENING GRILLS
CHILDRENS BEER GARDEN
← LUNCHES

Photo contributed by Michael Frank

The swings are OK, but the slide is rough on the catheter.

RESERVED FOR THE AGED AND HANDICAPPED

Photo contributed by John Talbott

Our Mission: Clothing the Hungry and Feeding the Naked

Photo contributed by Falconer

Oh sure, then heart problems will run for office, too.

Photo contributed by Bob Harrigan

For the closest thing to vegetables, it's . . .

Photo contributed by Nancy and David Berman

Even with a busted fin they still bite.

Photo contributed by S. J. Peters

Wimps Out for Minnows

Photo contributed by John O'Callaghan

The lights on their hats distract the bartender.

Photo contributed by
Lewis R. Harper

From the Truth in Advertising Department, Part I

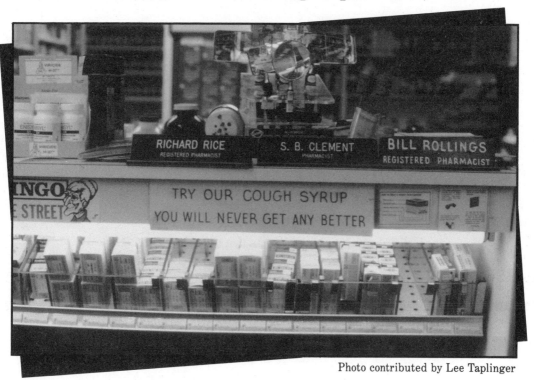

Photo contributed by Lee Taplinger

Swell Places to Eat and Sleep

Photo contributed by R. MacRae

Photo contributed by Steven and Wendy Schauder

Praise the Lord and pass the peanuts.

Photo contributed by Philippe Meilleur

Did you want hot sauce on that doctorate?

Photo contributed by Oswald F. Angst

The Better Part of Valor

Photo contributed by Oswald F. Angst

You'll be the first to know.

Photo contributed by Tom R. Porter III

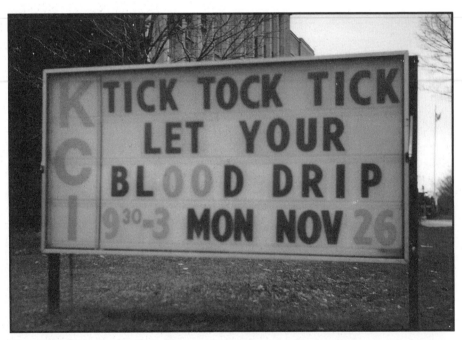

Photo contributed by David G. Lynn

Photo contributed by Daniel Santolini

Popes in Retirement

Photo contributed by David Bateman

Photo contributed by Randy Wood

Subliminal Substances

Photo contributed
by Michelle Hansen

Photo contributed by Avery Frost

Photo contributed by Judy Lalley

Wit or windstorm?

Photo contributed by Tom Gallagher

Photo contributed by Donald R. Shreier

When you're tired of life . . .

Photo contributed by Michael Grissom

Photo contributed by Ralph Doty

Photo contributed by Nicole Bassett

Front-row seats for the three-hanky puppy funeral

Photo contributed by Robert Hatcher

Opie vs. *Death Wish*

OFFICIAL PRIMARY BALLOT REPUBLICAN PARTY PASCO COUNTY, FLORIDA October 2, 1990		
STATE		
COMMISSIONER OF AGRICULTURE	**CHARLES BRONSON**	99 ➡
—Vote for ONE—	**RON HOWARD**	100 ➡

Absentee ballot instructions from Pasco County, Florida;
contributed by Christina Renke

Just wipe your shoes before you come in, Phil.

Photo contributed by Thomas H. Bonte

You can Pfuhl some of the people some of the time . . .

Photo contributed by David Jackino

Photo contributed by Lisa Brandt

MISSI G, Part I

Photo contributed by Linda Sherbert

Photo contributed by James M. Ford

. . . and you've got the place all to yourselves.

Photo contributed by Philip A. Wood

Equal Opportunity Employers

Photo contributed by Margaret Jarvie

Vanquish them until they learn.

Photo contributed by Tom Dorman

And what a swell team it must be.

Photo contributed by Gail Folda

Compulsory School—the Case in Favor

Photo contributed by R. J. Swanson

Photo contributed by Dierdre Serio

Eat and die.

Photo contributed by Chad Miller

Freshly Squeezed

Photo contributed by Richard Deight

Caution: Allow ample time to lower lifeboats when scheduling emergencies.

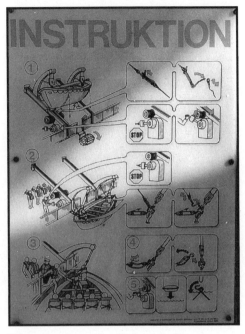

Photo contributed by Richard L. Turner

You can't even pitch a tent on it.

Photo contributed by Mike Gonzalez

Photo contributed by Damon Foster

Get in the car, kids, Daddy has a surprise!

Photo contributed by Sherrie Roden

So show some respect, you.

Photo contributed by David D. Jarvis

Photo contributed by Wendy Cowdon

Photo contributed by Liz Lindsey

Confucius says . . .

Photo contributed by Chris Van Hasselt

Emergencies only.

Photo contributed by Nuhki Ciammi

Look, honey, they're having a sale today!

Photo contributed by Larry Koepsell

Photo contributed by Joel Rubenstein

I agree with his politics, but he seems to have an inferiority complex.

Photo contributed
by Michael Nigro

Photo contributed by Lori Irving

Photo contributed by
H. D. Meatwagon

Plates? Wow, who won the lottery?!

Ad on a building in Brooklyn, New York;
photo contributed by Thomas M. Callahan

We're a small but proud town.

Photo contributed by John Naas

Let's just say the sheriff doesn't want any trouble around here.

Photo contributed by Pedar Ness

Adults only, please.

Photo contributed by Dave Law

Photo contributed by Karen McGillivray

Photo contributed by Peter Lorenz

Photo contributed by Chuck Prosek

Photo contributed by Elizabeth Sims

From the *San Diego Tribune*; contributed by Tony Slad

I guess everyone has their own interpretation of the Bible.

Photo contributed by Wendy Cowden

CHINCA'S MARKET
NO-NO'S

1. NO RESTROOM PRIVILEGES IN PHONE BOOTH
2. NO LITTERING
3. NO HANGING AROUND LOT
4. NO LOUD OR UNNECESSARY NOISES
5. NO DOPE DEALS ON LOT
6. NO DRINKING ALCOHOL ON PREMISES

OR YOU WILL BE ASKED TO MOVE ON

Pete Chinca

Photo contributed by Mike Troy

From the *Sacramento* (California) *Bee*; contributed by Joe Milton

43

Photo contributed by Alan Rose

Photo contributed by John Harris

Quick, who's got a quarter?

Photo contributed by Michael Viapiana

Photo contributed
by Frank Brennan

Photo contributed by
Thomas A. Ward

Photo contributed by Teri Plotnick

Sex Ed. 101.

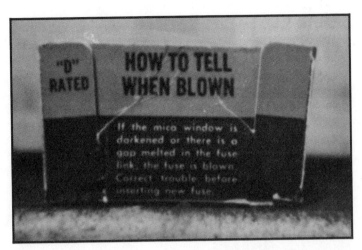

Photo contributed by Tony Scheuren

Boy, it sure pays to advertise!

Photo contributed by Robert Smyre

Small-town entertainment.

Oh no, it's Tony Danza!

Photo contributed by Pedar Ness

Photo contributed by Clark Risley

The power of persuasion.

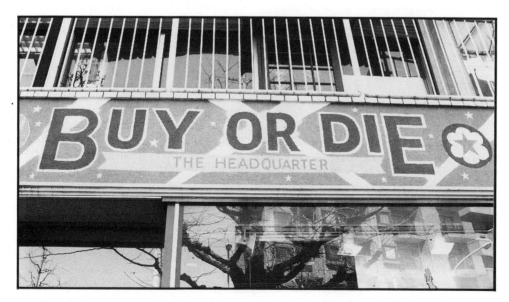

Photo contributed by Gary Curtis

Hmm, that's the fourth guy today asking for Cissy.

Photo contributed by Pedar Ness

Photo contributed by James Lola

Photo contributed by Steve Jones

161

Photo contributed by Joe Bissin

Photo contributed by
Mark S. Brzezniak

We were getting some complaints.

Photo contributed by Julia T. Momenko

Headless hollow, guaranteed solid heads, or oral sex prohibited?

Photo contributed by Brian S. Sheldon

. . . but do they float?

Photo contributed by Diana Schwabe

Self-Multiplying Automobile

Photo contributed by Max Apeture

Photo contributed by Doug Smith

Photo contributed by John Purcell

From the Random Monument Department

ON THIS SITE
IN 1897 NOTHING
HAPPENED.

Photo contributed by Gene Sorkin

$300 REWARD

FOR INFORMATION LEADING TO THE RETURN OF THIS LOST PET

NAME: MISIA (ME-SHA)

TYPE: RUSSIAN BLUE

SEX: FEMALE; SPAYED

AGE: 8 YEARS

COLOR: BLUE GREY BODY; GREEN EYES

LOST: MONDAY, OCTOBER 19; CASTRO & 15 TH STREETS

NOTE: MISIA IS UNDER-GOING CHEMO-THERAPY TREAT-MENT AND NEEDS HER MEDICATION

CALL: ▮▮▮▮▮▮▮▮

It even reads for you.

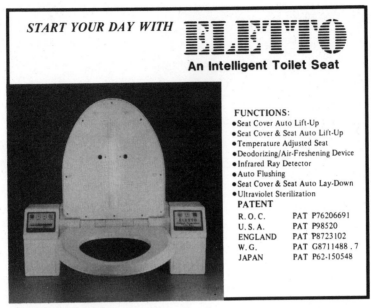

From an unidentified magazine;
contributed by Ron Ramsden

Photo contributed by Don Williams

News You
Can Abuse

. . . and after we nab 'em, we squash 'em with this here roller.

The Delta police department is in the middle of its Spring CounterAttack program, but that doesn't mean it's turning a blind eye to other offences. Here, police officers use a radar gun to nab speeding motorists.

From the *Delta* (British Columbia) *Optimist*; contributed by Gordon Felotick

Just don't wash the dog in it.

Peculiar water safe to drink
Boiling order lifted by state

PECULIAR — Residents can once again drink from their water faucets without fear.

The Missouri Department of Natural Resources lifted an order suggesting that Peculiar residents boil water for five minutes before drinking it. The DNR placed the boil order Thursday, after a vehicle struck a fire hydrant, knocking the hydrant loose.

"The boil order is off and everything is all right," said Ray England, utility superintendent of Peculiar.

From the *Belton* (Missouri) *Star-Herald*;
contributed by Julia Hylander

. . . and it didn't look so great on TV either.

Bloody butt hurts Ramirez

Chavez still unbeaten in 62 pro fights

From the *Lahaina* (Hawaii) *News*;
contributed by D. Hunter Bishop

It's a Wonderful Day in the Neighborhood

● A 64-year-old on the 1100 block of Santa Fe Avenue reported that when he left his house at 8:15 a.m. April 5 his windows were clean and when he returned at 11 a.m. they were dirty.

He said his next-door neighbor, a 66-year-old woman, had spit on them. He claimed to have photos of her spitting on his windows in the past.

The neighbor called him a bastard and said she spits on his windows only when he throws things on her roof. The officer saw window stained and also saw refuse on the woman's roof. The man said he only throws things on her roof after she throws things in his backyard.

From the
San Diego (California) *Tribune*;
contributed by Lisa Pasqua

● AN ITALIAN who had been injured in a traffic accident was placed on a stretcher which rolled out the back of an ambulance that was rushing him to a hospital in Avellino. On reaching the hospital, the driver discovered his patient was no longer in the vehicle. The patient hitchhiked the rest of the way to the hospital and was treated for his injuries.

From the Albany, California, *Journal*;
contributed by Mary Thomson

At 9 p.m., a Oak Harbor resident reported his neighbor has been placing his dog on the hood of his car and driving approximately 70 m.p.h. The neighbor told the complainant the dog loved it.

From the *Whidbey News-Times*,
Oak Harbor, Washington;
contributed by Ritchard W. Brown

To hospital — Longview police took a 41-year-old Longview man to St. John's Medical Center for mental health assistance Sunday after it was reported he was behaving strangely at his home on 17th Avenue. Police were told he had washed himself with motor oil and cleaned his trailer with tomato juice Sunday.

From the Longview, Washington, *Daily News*; contributed by Darren Day

Corn Country Excitement

From the *Cedar Rapids Gazette*;
contributed by Bill Irwin

Toward Increased Global Warming

HOW WOMEN'S TOP 25 FARTED

How the Associated Press' Top 25 women's teams fared this week:

■ 1. Virginia (27-2) did not play. beat North Carolina 90-69; lost to Clemson 65-62.

■ 2. Penn State (26-1) did not play. beat No. 24 George Washington 77-62. beat St. Joseph's 76-40.

■ 3. Georgia (26-3) did not play. beat South Alabama 125-64; beat Alabama 78-69. lost to No. 12 LSU 83-74.

■ 4. Tennessee (25-4) did not play. beat Vanderbilt 62-60; beat No. 5 Auburn 70-62.

■ 5. Auburn (24-5) did not play. beat No. 18 Mississippi 76-50. lost to No. 4 Tennessee 70-62.

■ 6. Purdue (24-2) did not play. beat Illinois 112-49.

■ 7. North Carolina State (25-5) did not play. beat E. Carolina 116-73. beat Wake Forest 92-72. beat Maryland 82-75.

■ 8. Arkansas (24-3) did not play. beat Baylor 90-74.

■ 9. Washington (21-4) beat UCLA 64-54.

■ 10. Stanford (22-4) did not play. beat California 93-80;

■ 11. Western Kentucky (25-2) did not play. beat Old Dominion 73-63; beat Virginia Commonwealth 102-84.

■ 12. LSU (23-6) did not play. beat No. 19 Stephen F. Austin 79-77. beat Kentucky 96-76; beat No. 3 Georgia 83-74.

■ 13. Connecticut (25-4) did not play. beat Pittsburgh 79-55; beat Villanova 64-47; beat Seton Hall 69-54.

■ 14. Texas (20-7) did not play. beat Texas Tech 77-53. beat Texas Christian 77-40. beat Southern Methodist 90-52.

■ 15. UNLV (24-5) did not play. beat Fresno State 72-69; beat Pacific 102-76.

■ 16. Providence (25-4) did not play. beat Villanova 74-69. beat Georgetown 95-91; beat Pittsburgh 107-92.

■ 17. Rutgers (22-5) did not play. beat St. Joseph's 73-51. lost to West Virginia 89-78.

■ 18. Mississippi (20-8) did not play. beat Mississippi State 74-56. lost to No. 5 Auburn, 76-50.

■ 19. Stephen F. Austin (23-4) did not play. lost to No. 12 LSU 79-77. beat McNeese State 101-41.

■ 20. Northwestern (19-7) did not play. beat Indiana 87-71; beat Ohio State 71-55.

■ 21. Iowa (18-8) did not play. beat Louisiana Tech 72-57. beat Michigan 76-64. lost to Michigan State 49-48.

■ 22. Notre Dame (21-6) did not play. lost to Dayton 79-76. beat Xavier-Ohio 69-53.

■ 23. Long Beach State (19-7) did not play. beat Pacific 91-73. beat San Jose State, 73-53.

■ 24. George Washington (22-5) did not play. lost to No. 2 Penn State 77-62. beat St. Bonaventure, 84-59.

■ 25. Lamar (25-2) did not play.

From the *Boulder* (Colorado) *Daily Camera*;
contributed by Alan Hlava

Pissing policeman loses handgun to 2 holdupmen

Two unidentified men reportedly armed with a handgun and a fan knife took the service revolver of a Quezon City policeman who was urinating in a vacant lot near a shopping mall in Mandaluyong Wednesday night.

The policeman was identified as Pat. Chito Aquino, 38, detailed with Station 4 of the Central Police District, of 1930 Mount Apo st., Punta, Sta. Ana, Manila.

Aquino told Mandaluyong police probers that the robbery happened at around 11:20 p.m. in a vacant lot between the EDSA Central mall and the Melvin department store.

Police said Aquino, who had been drinking that night, did not notice the two suspects approach as he was urinating.

Aquino lost only his Smith and Wesson .38 cal. revolver to the two unidentified men, who fled towards Shaw blvd. after the robbery. (Jun Burgos)

From the *Manila* (Philippines) *Standard*;
contributed by Christopher Landrum

Anatomical Tidings

Colon outburst highlights trial

BOSTON — In an outburst during the second day of his U.S. District Court trial on narcotics trafficking charges, a Fitchburg man leaped to his feet and shouted denials of government claims that he operated a cocaine distribution operation from his Worcester convenience store.

"I no sell drugs!" cried 37-year-old Rafael Colon of 14 Pleasant St., Fitchburg as court officers hurried to restrain him.

From the *Fitchburg* (Massachusetts) *Sentinel & Enterprise*;
contributed by Bruce Siart

Boner rises, shines after inauguration gala

From the *Nashville Banner*;
contributed by Matt Bolch

Venereal disease is linked to crack

From the *Altoona* (Pennsylvania) *Mirror*;
contributed by Denis Navarro

Men picky about noses

From the *New Orleans Times-Picayune*;
contributed by Susan D. Indest

61

The parties are fun, but those things really look funny in the refrigerator.

Sex gadgets are replacing Tupperware

From the *Cleveland Plain Dealer*;
contributed by Eric Ambro

And the Bubonic Award goes to . . .

First State Capitol Day Held

Senator Phil Rock, (with plague), being presented the Distinquished Service Award by Ted Scharle, Bradley; Constance Cavany, U of I Urbana; Don Koehn, Illinois Wesleyan; Conley Stutz, Bradley; Art Robinson, U of I Urbana.

From *Illinois Academe*;
contributed by D. S. Knutson

Sesame Spite

Arriving at Hirsch Coliseum March 5 are Sesame Street stars
The Cunt, (clockwise from top left) Grover, Big Bird, Cookie
Monster, Oscar the Grouch, Prairie Dawn, Ernie and Bert.

From the *Shreveport* (Louisiana) *Times*;
contributed by Susan Parmer

Just remove the toilet paper and we'll keep an eye on you.

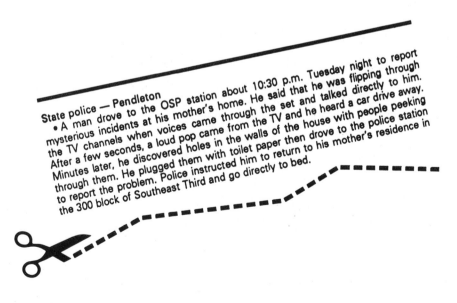

State police — Pendleton
• A man drove to the OSP station about 10:30 p.m. Tuesday night to report mysterious incidents at his mother's home. He said that he was flipping through the TV channels when voices came through the set and talked directly to him. After a few seconds, a loud pop came from the TV and he heard a car drive away. Minutes later, he discovered holes in the walls of the house with people peeking through them. He plugged them with toilet paper then drove to the police station to report the problem. Police instructed him to return to his mother's residence in the 300 block of Southeast Third and go directly to bed.

From the *East Oregonian*;
contributed by Gus Mortier

Enduring Problems

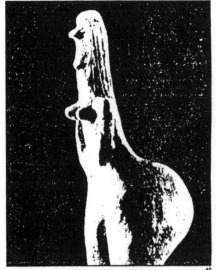

Juxtaposed in the Syracuse, New York, *Post-Standard*; contributed by Steven R. King

Movie rights, anyone?

Car-bug collision destroys vehicle

The Times-Mail

PAOLI — A Paoli woman miraculously escaped injury when her car flipped after she was blinded when a large bug hit her outside mirror and splattered onto her face and glasses.

The Orange County Sheriff's Department said the 1982 Subaru driven by Peggy Lee, 40, ran off the side of the road and flipped at 11:59 a.m. Lee was four to five miles east of Paoli on U.S. 150. The car was a total loss.

From the Bedford, Indiana, *Times-Mail*; contributed by Bradley Wayne Kalnajs

What good are they empty?

Public input on condoms sought

Page 3

From the *Edmonton* (Alberta, Canada) *Examiner*;
contributed by David Berger

Flip a coin.

2 Towns Vie For Pizza Hut Sewage

Raritan Township's sewer authority and Flemington are still arguing over which municipality gets to process sewage from an as-yet unbuilt Pizza Hut.

The restaurant has been approved for a vacant tract next to the Flemington Mall that is on the boundary line between the two towns.

According to Gregory Watts, the authority's attorney, the bulk of the property is in Flemington, but the authority has a sewer line that bisects the property and the developer would like to hook into that line.

However, the line then runs through a section of the borough before returning to the township and at no time passes through the Flemington metering station.

The borough planning board has already approved Pizza Hut's request to build. Councilman George Wilson has been insisting that Flemington receive the sewer connection and service charges from the property.

It's the authority view that since sewage from that line wouldn't pass through the borough meter, Flemington wouldn't be charged by the authority. And authority members have said they don't intend to give services away.

At last Wednesday's authority meeting, Watts reiterated the position that since it owns and maintains the line, the authority is entitled to all the fees Pizza Hut would have to pay.

The two groups will meet again to discuss the situation again, but no date has been set.

From the *Hunterdon County* (New Jersey) *Democrat*;
contributed by Diana Schwabe

Shit saves thief

By Lucas Lukumbo of *Shihata*

A SUSPECTED thief smeared his body with his own shit to deter arrest, it has been learnt.

The suspect whose name was not immediately known stole a pair of trousers from a resident along Upanga Road in the city and ran towards the Indian Ocean when people spotted him.

An eyewitness Ndugu Denis Magubila told *Shihata* that the thief was caught at the Gymkhana Golf grounds and was forced to untire the trouser he had already worn inside his worn-out trouser.

Ndugu Magubila said that the thief who seemed to respond the demands of the people to untire the trouser 'kept silent for some minutes forcing himself to shit, and took the shit with his hands and smeared himself with it leaving the people dump-founded.

Nobody could arrest the already smelling middle-aged thief who ran towards the Indian Ocean shore apparently to take a bath.

From the *Daily News* of Dar Es Salaam, Tanzania; contributed by Thomas Hettel

Colon accused of shoplifting condoms

From the *Columbia* (Missouri) *Daily Tribune*; contributed by Chuck Lay

Boner big winner in women's city

From the *Elkhart* (Indiana) *Truth*; contributed by Chris Edwards

Ohio flood toll rises to 15; dozens missing

SHADYSIDE, Ohio (AP) — Searchers recovered the bodies of four people Saturday, bringing to 15 the confirmed death toll from a flash flood that raged through eastern Ohio, authorities said. About three dozen people remained missing.

A 5-year-old Glencoe girl, Tiffany Webb, was found dead in McMahon Creek early Saturday, said Chuck Vogt, Belmont County coroner's investigator. The girl and her 6-year-old brother, Donald Andrew Webb, were killed when Thursday night's flood swept their mobile home from its concrete mooring.

Later in the day, Vogt reported two additional victims, Danny Humphrey, 8, hometown unknown, and Mary Grimes, age and hometown unknown. A fourth victim, who was not identified, was discovered in the Ohio River late in the afternoon, Vogt said last night.

Capt. Jim Boling of the Ohio Air National Guard said the number of people missing was revised Saturday evening to 34. Previous reports from Belmont County authorities had given the number as 51.

New water manager getting his feet wet

By Thom Akeman
Herald Staff Writer

Jim Cofer has been getting his feet wet for a month now, wading through the problems of the Monterey Peninsula Water Man-

(Herald photo)
JIM COFER

agement District.

So far, he said, he's decided that he needs to set priorities so he doesn't get bogged down.

"I'm trying not to get too sidetracked on rationing and all these interim problems. They could overwhelm us," Cofer said during an interview. "I want to make sure we set our priorities and keep them straight."

The new general manager of the water district said his basic goal will be to enlarge the water supply on the Monterey Peninsula.

He said he is now working his way through the massive environmental impact report for water allocation on the Peninsula and trying to figure out the status of the EIR for a possible dam on the Carmel River.

And as soon as he gets around to it, there are 15 cartons waiting in the corner of his new office, cartons filled with files that former manager Bruce Buel left behind for him to read.

"There's more than I anticipated," Cofer said. "I'm clearly

(Continued on page 4A)

Side-by-side articles in the Monterey, California, *Morning Herald*; contributed by Marci Padfield

. . . and he'll damned well do what he's told.

Hachette Names Pecker To Run U.S. Magazines

By a WALL STREET JOURNAL *Staff Reporter*

NEW YORK—Hachette S.A., putting its U.S. magazine operations under the control of an American executive for the first time, named David J. Pecker executive vice president/publishing of the Paris-based media giant's Hachette Magazines Inc. unit.

From the *Wall Street Journal*; contributed by Christopher Chaloux

. . . while feet head for county line.

Hand waves goodbye to county board

By Ed Tagliaferri
Staff Writer

John Hand, whose low-key leadership helped tame a sometimes volatile Westchester County Board of Legislators, will not run for re-election in November.

John Hand

Hand, the board's chairman since January 1990 and a legislator for 18 years, said yesterday in a written statement that he would not seek a 10th term so as to "make way for a new generation of leaders who will take our county into the next century."

"Ecclesiastes tells us that there is a time for everything. Well, this is the time for John Hand to step down," he said.

From the Westchester County, New York, *Citizen-Register*; contributed anonymously

. . . with special emphasis on turnips.

SDSU Adds to Staff

BROOKINGS — South Dakota State University has added two new staff members.

Brent Turnipseed has been named director of the SDSU Seed Lab. He is a native of Minnesota and is finishing his Ph.D. at Mississippi State University. He will also be teaching and leading seed research activities.

Brent Turnipseed

From a South Dakota newspaper;
contributed by Kim Korth

Body search reveals $4,000 in crack

From the *Jackson* (Michigan) *Citizen-Patriot*;
contributed by Tom Oswald

And now for the local news . . .

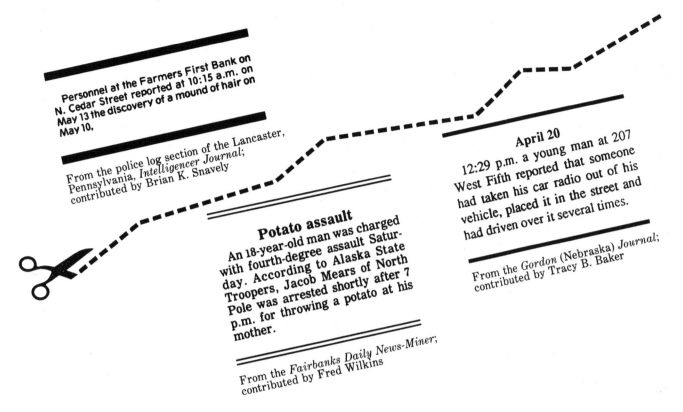

Personnel at the Farmers First Bank on N. Cedar Street reported at 10:15 a.m. on May 13 the discovery of a mound of hair on May 10,

From the police log section of the Lancaster, Pennsylvania, *Intelligencer Journal*; contributed by Brian K. Snavely

Potato assault

An 18-year-old man was charged with fourth-degree assault Saturday. According to Alaska State Troopers, Jacob Mears of North Pole was arrested shortly after 7 p.m. for throwing a potato at his mother.

From the *Fairbanks Daily News-Miner*; contributed by Fred Wilkins

April 20

12:29 p.m. a young man at 207 West Fifth reported that someone had taken his car radio out of his vehicle, placed it in the street and had driven over it several times.

From the *Gordon* (Nebraska) *Journal*; contributed by Tracy B. Baker

Getting paid for what they do best.

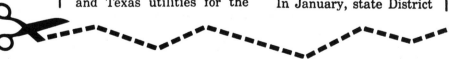

County wants money for taking dump

By Suzanne Gamboa
Associated Press

SIERRA BLANCA, Texas — Hudspeth County should be compensated by the state and Texas utilities for the happened we lost all our negotiating power," he said.

The utilities aren't willing to make any payments until they know the dump's location is permanent.

The state initially proposed building the dump in Fort Hancock, about 60 miles east of Downtown El Paso, and now is studying the area near Sierra Blanca, about 90 miles east of Downtown.

In January, state District

From the *El Paso Times*; contributed by Daniel J. Wiley

Try plant food.

Police ask for tips on marijuana growing

LOWVILLE — Lewis County Sheriff's deputies want the community's help to find people who grew marijuana plants in the town of West Turin.

Sixty plants, each about 4 feet tall, were found yesterday in a remote area of the town. The plants were cut down.

People with information should call the department at 376-3511.

From the *Utica* (New York) *Observer-Dispatch*;
contributed by Steve Holstein

CORRECTIONS

A Thursday story incorrectly quoted Councilman Stewart Clifton as calling Mayor Bill Boner a "squeeze-bag." Clifton called Boner a "sleaze-bag."

From the *Nashville Banner*;
contributed by Mike Long

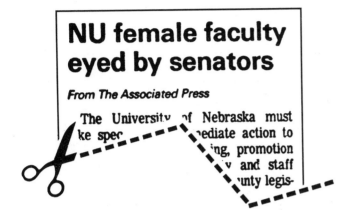

NU female faculty eyed by senators

From The Associated Press

The University of Nebraska must ke spec_____ediate action to _____ng, promotion _____ and staff _____unty legis-

From the *Lincoln* (Nebraska) *Journal-Star*;
contributed by Tom Ulrich

Cops Kill Music Fan

Jacksonville, Fla.

Police responding to complaints that Ronald Neil Boyd, 56, was playing Glenn Miller music too loud killed him in an exchange of gunfire that they say he started.

Associated Press

From the *San Francisco Chronicle*;
contributed by Marty Stuzinski

The Case for a Lawn Service

Wife says Weeding killed her husband

From the *San Diego Union*;
contributed by Jim Hopkins

. . . as witnessed by your local notority public.

The Eighties: Decade Of Notority

From the Stuart, Virginia, *Bull Mountain Bugle*; contributed by Beverly Dillard

Commissioner Davis To Head "Assault On Literacy Month"

From the *Pahokee* (Florida) *Sun*; contributed by Donald Vaughan

Sadness Is No. 1 Reason Men and Women Cry

From the *Omaha World Herald*; contributed by Josh Hamilton

April slated as child abuse month

Our mistake

Liberal MP Sheila Copps did not direct cries of "scumbag" at the Government benches in the House of Commons as reported yesterday. As recorded by Hansard, her comments were, "Who is a scumbag?" followed by, "The honorable member just called us a scumbag."

A Nov. 9 Southam News story about Nova Scotia's black minority was accompanied by an inaccurate photograph caption. The photo, said to depict rundown homes outside Dartmouth, was actually of a pig farm. *The Citizen* apologises for the error.

Correction

The mock penile implant precedure pictured on Monday's Close-Up page was photographed at Mercy Hospital, not, as the cutline read, at Baystate Medical Center.

Carbon man sets himself on fire

From the (Allentown, Pennsylvania) *Morning Call*; contributed by H. D. Klopp

Bad diapers draw crowd

Fire damage heavy to Torch Oil Co.

Iran Claims Success In Its Attacks On Iran

Women protest charge of causing drought

NIAMEY, Niger — Hundreds of women marched yesterday to protest being harassed by people who blame them for a shortage of rainfall in this impoverished nation on the fringes of the Sahara Desert.

The march was organized by the Niger Women's Association and the Niger Human Rights Association after some young women wearing short skirts were blamed for the drought and stripped in public.

Men who falsely claim to be Muslim holy men, known here as marabouts, have asserted that the women's dress was responsible for the lower-than-normal rainfall this year.

Police also interrogated women whose clothes were deemed indecent.

Church Retains Homosexual Bar

Mother of disabled student charges aide with battery

Navy Apologizes for Tying Sailor to Blast

From the *Los Angeles Times*; contributed by Mitch Giannunzio

74

Multiple-personality rapist sentenced to two life terms

From the Greensboro (North Carolina) News & Record; contributed by Lee Vernon

Relief groups help hurt family

From the Escondido (California) Times-Advocate; contributed by Marianne Roberts

The Thurlows, *pictured here with their daughter Madelaine, were watching* St. Elsewhere *on television when their house in Birmingham, England, caught fire. A fireman said that Mrs. Thurlow and her two daughters continued watching the show as the house burned around them. "One of the daughters was smoking a cigarette. The wife was coughing." Firefighters removed the three women, a dog, and a "big fluffy cat" without injury.* From the Baltimore Evening Sun; contributed by J. Dimeler

Rejected boyfriend kills pets

POMPANO BEACH, Fla. (AP) — A man angry over a broken romance killed his ex-girlfriend's pet birds, stole her cat and stomped her daughter's bunny to death, police said.

Daniel R. Baxter, 35, was being held Tuesday at the Broward County Jail in lieu of $50,000 bail on charges of burglary and theft and cruelty to animals.

During the past few weeks, Kim Long reported two of her birds had been killed and two were missing. And a neighbor reported seeing Baxter take Long's cat, which has not been found, authorities said.

Baxter showed up a short time later at a Fort Lauderdale restaurant where Ms. Long works and was arrested after smashing her windshield, police said.

Senator Slips Pork to City

■ Tarky Lombardi kept a $600,000 grant to Syracuse under wraps until the state legislative session adjourned. He was afraid Cuomo might kill the measure.

By LUTHER F. BLIVEN
Albany Bureau

A surprise $600,000 legislative grant for the city of Syracuse will be unveiled today by state Sen. Tarky Lombardi at a news conference in Syracuse.

The previously unannounced allocation was tucked away in one of the last-minute budget cleanup and supplemental spending bills passed by lawmakers in the closing hours of last week's windup meeting for the 1992 legislative session.

State Sen. Tarky Lombardi got a windfall for Syracuse.
File photo

The grant was so closely guarded that some Syracuse-area legislators won't know they voted for it until Lombardi's news conference today. The Syracuse Republican kept the appropriation secret until the legislative session was over for fear Gov. Mario Cuomo would get wind of the allocation and ax it before lawmakers left town.

The money will help ease Syracuse through a major fiscal crisis that has plagued Mayor Tom Young for months and which could have resulted in a sizable budget deficit by the end of the year.

The city's award-winning "Safe Streets" program was used as the hook on which to hang the $600,000 allocation.

"The monies would be used to continue the city's highly successful 'Safe Streets' or 'Team Oriented Policing' program, which is now operating in city neighborhoods," Lombardi said. Officers in the program operate out of a trailer that moves to different neighborhoods to help residents solve problems involving crime, housing and social services.

The $600,000 grant will free up city money now used for the police program to finance something else, Lombardi said.

The senator said the $600,000 replaces a similar amount Young had expected to receive from a proposed horse-racing theater. The city had asked Syracuse-area legislators to sponsor a bill authorizing a public referendum on the theater. The first $416,000 of betting revenues from the theater were to be earmarked for the arts.

(See LOMBARDI, Page A-4)

From the (Syracuse) *Post-Standard*; contributed by Casey J. Dickinson

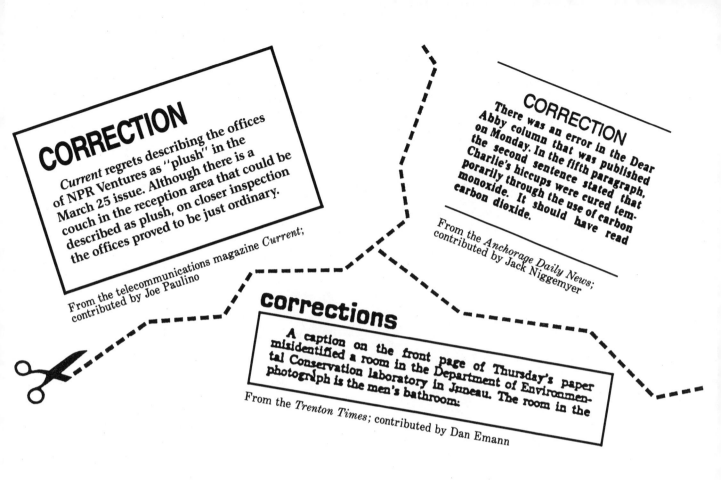

CORRECTION

Current regrets describing the offices of NPR Ventures as "plush" in the March 25 issue. Although there is a couch in the reception area that could be described as plush, on closer inspection the offices proved to be just ordinary.

From the telecommunications magazine *Current;* contributed by Joe Paulino

CORRECTION

There was an error in the Dear Abby column that was published on Monday. In the fifth paragraph, the second sentence stated that Charlie's hiccups were cured temporarily through the use of carbon monoxide. It should have read carbon dioxide.

From the *Anchorage Daily News;* contributed by Jack Niggemyer

corrections

A caption on the front page of Thursday's paper misidentified a room in the Department of Environmental Conservation laboratory in Juneau. The room in the photograph is the men's bathroom.

From the *Trenton Times;* contributed by Dan Emann

Teen Jailed in Snatch

Stripper resents exposure

Ball a bag lady in 'Stone Pillow'

Landlords evict Supreme Court

From the (Fredonia, New York) *Leader*; contributed by Brian Telander

Despite the poor weather conditions, the Devils held their own against Houghton.

Boss is coming, quick, hide that thing!

Marijuana found in tuna can

ARDSLEY, N.Y. (AP) — The black spot in the can of tuna made Rita Shafer curious. What looked like a partially smoked marijuana cigarette on the lid made her incredulous.

"I couldn't believe it was there," Shafer said Wednesday, the day after she opened the can of Bumble Bee albacore tuna to make lunch for her 3-year-old daughter Brandi.

Bumble Bee can't quite believe it, either, and a spokeswoman said the company wants to look at the can.

"We've never had anything like this happen," said Deborah Streeter, administrator of consumer affairs for Bumble Bee. "It's very serious, if it's true. We've taken the code and we're tracking where and when it was packed." The can was sealed in California.

Bumble Bee asked her to send the can back to its headquarters in San Diego.

No recall was contemplated at this time, Streeter said.

Streeter said the company has stringent quality control standards and such an incident is unlikely. She said the tuna is still safe because the product goes through a heat sterilization process to kill germs and bacteria.

Shafer said she figured someone either put it in the can as a joke or was stealing a smoke and had to hide it because someone was coming his way.

The incident "really blew my mind," she added.

Screw 'em if they can't take a joke.

Bus driver who hit dog quits job

PORT WASHINGTON, Wis. (AP) — A school bus driver insists he was joking when he shouted "Should I hit the dog?" moments before running over the animal that belonged to two of his young passengers.

The 44-year-old driver quit Thursday while the Ozaukee County district attorney considered a recommendation by the sheriff's office to file a charge of animal mistreatment. Sheriff's Lt. Keith Gross said investigators concluded the man ran over the dog intentionally Jan. 26.

Among nine students on the bus were two children whose family owned the dog, a 17-month-old Brittany spaniel named Chelsea.

Melissa Monahan, mother of the 9-year-old girl and 11-year-old boy said the dog often came up to the road when it saw the bus.

From the *Cedar Rapids Daily Tribune*; contributed by Dale Bowden

From the (Medford, Oregon) *Mail Tribune*; contributed by R. J. Holmes

The Folger Consort will be hard at 10 a.m. Christmas Day.

City to control beaver with contraceptive

Associated Press

WHEAT RIDGE — A female beaver, too young to breed and establish her own lodge on Clear Creek, has lost her reproductive chance after being fitted with a Norplant contraceptive device.

Littleton veterinarian David Robinson performed the implant Thursday — the first such sterilization of a beaver in the state.

The city of Wheat Ridge, eager to find a humane method of controlling beaver populations, teamed up with Wildlife 2000, an environmental group working with the Colorado Division of Wildlife to experiment with beaver contraception.

"It just took a few minutes and was far less painful than if she had been given a tubal ligation, which we have done to sterilize beaver in the past," Wildlife 2000 president Sherri Tippie said.

Who says the Swiss never contribute anything to mankind?

● A SWISS inventor tests his hinged bicycle in Zurich. The inventor, who sensibly prefers that his name not be used, said the idea seemed to make sense when he thought of it. But, after riding it, he admits it makes no sense. He added: "We live in a world where every little thing is supposed to make sense, and I'm tired of that."

Photo contributed by Sherrie Roden

Members of Gay Men's Chorus of Los Angeles, who usually wear tuxedos for concerts, don expressive costumes for "Hidden Legacies" performances.

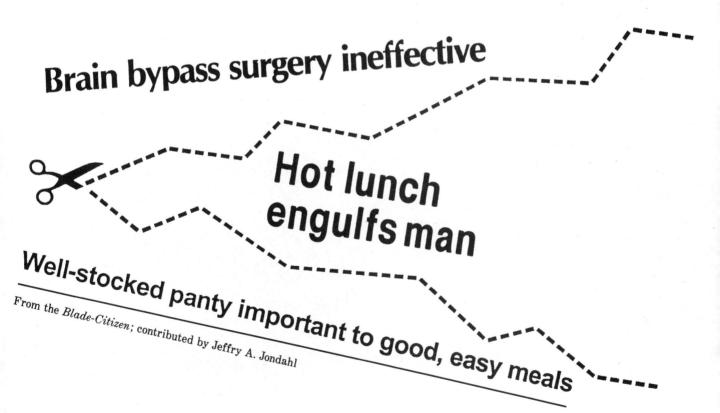

Brain bypass surgery ineffective

Hot lunch
engulfs man

Well-stocked panty important to good, easy meals

From the *Blade-Citizen*; contributed by Jeffry A. Jondahl

CORRECTION

In the story Saturday about animal control work in Paso Robles, the featured quotation was incorrectly attributed to Robert Dollahite, director of the county Animal Regulation Department.

That statement, "I drive to work everyday watching dead cats getting flatter and flatter" was actually made by Richard Deming, Paso Robles city manager.

From the San Luis Obispo County Telegram-Tribune; contributed by Toni Spencer

Correction

A story about parolee Newt Becknell in Sunday's *Enquirer* incorrectly said that he was married. By an editing error, Becknell was described as single.

Corrections

A story in Sunday editions stated that parolee Newt Becknell is married. He is single. A correction Monday failed to make that clear.

From two consecutive issues of the Cincinnati Enquirer; contributed by Rosanna Hoberg

CORRECTION

Due to an error in transcription, Danielle Brisebois was misrepresented in *US* ("Where Are They Now?" *US* 60). Discussing the demands of the acting profession, Brisebois was misquoted as saying, "You have to know how to run, you have to be in shape, you have to know how to do sex acts." She actually said, "You have to know how to do circus acts." *US* regrets the error.

From US magazine; contributed by David Masella

From the Edmonton (Kentucky) Herald News; contributed by Peter Acree

Albert Francis was the knobby knee winner and Alma Parrigan won the hog calling contest.

Items that are round and wrinkled stand out among nutritious foods

Boner pops up in Mickey Mouse march

Contributed by Scott Rouse

Szoka plans drive for priests to climax during pope's visit

From the *Detroit Free Press*; contributed by Tim Hamlin

**Whoa, slow down, doc,
so those of us without a medical degree can keep up with you.**

**Dr. J.F. Phelps, Chiropractor
Palmer Graduate**

Using the Toilet (Seated)

Draw the foot of the long leg back by about the length of the foot. Alternatively, sit with the toes of both feet aligned symmetrically. When using the toilet there is a tendency towards extreme bending in the angles of hip joints and care must be taken with regard to the placing of the feet...use the paper from the side on which the leg is long.

From the *Gwinnet* (Michigan) *Daily News*; contributed by Mark R. Coulston

I swear, that man doesn't look a day over 75.

Dick Clark, seen here at age 92, gets three hours of airtime on two networks

If Astros win, will they come?

BY GENE DUFFEY
OF THE HOUSTON POST STAFF

The earth moved Sunday morning in California and still the fans made it to Dodger Stadium, 26,260 ignoring the earthquake and paying to see Los Angeles

From the Houston Post

Officials warn clams, oysters can carry virus

Shortage of Brains Slows Medical Research

See you next year, babe.

A family affair. A good time was had by all who attended the Celebrity Rodeo and Longhorn Cattle Drive.

Photo contributed by Anne Pellegrino

Quick, Larry, it's my only chance!——

Man beats off bear to save his friend

Democrats welcome Dicks this year at party's 'big love-in'

Almost as prestigious as the John Holmes Cup.

Record-setting Wang wins
Jesse Owens Trophy

From the *Duluth News-Tribune*; contributed by Jack Fiamoncini

My God, someone get this poor victim some counseling!

Holdup for pleasure

Canadian Press

MONTREAL — A man held a gun on a taxi driver while his female companion performed oral sex on the cabbie, police said. Provincial police said the cab driver told them the woman later tipped him $24. The 40-year-old cabbie, identified only as Michel, picked up a couple early Sunday in Chambly, south of Montreal.

He said the woman, in her 20s, who was sitting beside him on the front seat, propositioned him as he was driving, police said.

When he refused her advances, her male companion, who was in his 50s, pressed the barrel of a handgun to his head and ordered him to let the woman have her way.

The cabbie said he kept driving as the woman performed oral sex.

He was later ordered to drive to suburban Longueuil, where the couple got out.

The cabbie told police the woman paid the $26 fare with a $50 bill and told him to keep the change.

From the Canadian newspaper *The Province*; contributed by Kevin Vancancius

Thompson's pen is a sword

Peters to pull out of two city projects

By Jeff B. Hansen
News staff writer

company be allowed to discontinue work on two city projects.

In a separate prepared statement

fraud charges by city attorneys and the state Attorney General's Office.

unfair and biased articles .

From the *Birmingham* (Alabama) *News*; contributed by Steve Elliot

The joy of pubic worship

From the *St. Charles* (Missouri) *Journal*; contributed by Bob Swain

Feminist leader marketing head

Woman benefits from cancer

Clerk reports: Marriages are on the rise; clamming permits down

Disciples of Christ Name Interim Leader

From the *Los Angeles Times*; contributed by Mitch Giannunzio

Hookers plying the Liffey thrill the crowds

From the *Irish Press*; contributed by F. Corbin

Barter trade: Negros cocks for marijuana

From a Philippine newspaper; contributed by Lewis Brown

Let's keep it on the ground, please, people.

Ozone Threatens Safe Sex

From the *San Francisco Chronicle*;
contributed by Bill Horgos

Hey, somebody could get killed in there!

Missouri Gas Chamber Is Unsafe

From the *Macon* (Missouri) *Chronicle-Herald*;
contributed by Scott C. Jones

And it took a lot of nerve, too.

Big bucks bagged by Balls

Calvin Balls, left, and Doug Ball, right, show off their fine prizes, early Monday morning, at the Couch Cowboy Resort. There were a lot of deer reported this year and as Calvin said "It was like Dieppe out there."

From the *Wiarton* (Ontario) *Echo*; contributed by Roly Thomas

From the Authentic Bogus Headline Department

Fake Bogus passes suspected

At least two people are apparently circulating phony ski passes for Bogus Basin Recreation Area, according to the Boise County sheriff's office.

Boise County officials confirmed Saturday that they are investigating a case involving at least two suspects and an unknown quantity of phony passes.

They said no further information would be released until the 2-week-old investigation is completed.

Bogus Basin Marketing Director Jane Dechambeau said ski area personnel found some suspicious passes and turned them over to the sheriff's office for investigation.

From the Idaho Journal;
contributed by T. Tiersch

It's too noisy around here, sonny. We'll take ours to go.

No such thing as a free lunch

When planning your summer musical activities, kindly take care to read the fine print. Summerfest officials report that when the Madison folk rock band Free Hot Lunch appeared there last year, several senior citizens misread the calendar and mistakenly figured they were in for free chow. Though their songs are spicy, the band has nothing to do with food.

From the Milwaukee Journal;
contributed by Greg Reske

She died with her pants on.

Cotton briefs

Cotton friends regretted to hear of the death Tuesday of Mrs. Mattie Lou Nix of Camilla.

From the Pelham *(Florida)* Journal;
contributed by Christopher Ellrich

Who wants a congressman named Tou Tou anyway?

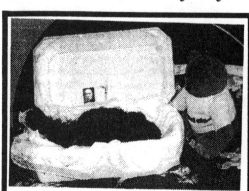

In memory of my best friend, Tou Tou who passed away April 17, 1989.
After 15 years of travelling all over the country with me I sure miss you dear friend.
I know you are up there in heaven.
If they decide to send you back, come back as you were, a beautiful little dog, not as a human being because they may make a mistake and send you back as a dirty, rotten, greedy, back-stabbing liar.
Rest in Peace Tou Tou
Herman and Tiger

From the Moncton *(New Brunswick, Canada)*
Times Transcript; contributed by R. Matthew

From the Which Way Is Up Department

Age of wisdom

Researchers at the University of Wales College in Cardiff are to spend two years trying to discover whether old people are really wiser than the young. A £65,000 project funded by the Economic and Social Research Council starts next year but the psychologists say they have to define what wisdom is first.

From the London *Daily Telegraph*;
contributed by Len Walker

Okay, so we all had a rotten day.

Seacoast Scorecard

Football

By The Associated Press
American Conference

East	W	L	T	Pct.	PF	PA
Buffalo	0	0	0	.000	00	00
Indianapolis	0	0	0	.000	00	00
Miami	0	0	0	.000	00	00
New England	0	0	0	.000	00	00
N.Y. Jets	0	0	0	.000	00	00
Central						
Cincinnati	0	0	0	.000	00	00
Cleveland	0	0	0	.000	00	00
Houston	0	0	0	.000	00	00
Pittsburgh	0	0	0	.000	00	00
West						
Denver	0	0	0	.000	00	00
Kansas City	0	0	0	.000	00	00
L.A. Raiders	0	0	0	.000	00	00
San Diego	0	0	0	.000	00	00
Seattle	0	0	0	.000	00	00

National Conference

East	W	L	T	Pct.	PF	PA
Dallas	0	0	0	.000	00	00
N.Y. Giants	0	0	0	.000	00	00
Philadelphia	0	0	0	.000	00	00
St. Louis	0	0	0	.000	00	00
Washington	0	0	0	.000	00	00
Central						
Chicago	0	0	0	.000	00	00
Detroit	0	0	0	.000	00	00
Green Bay	0	0	0	.000	00	00
Minnesota	0	0	0	.000	00	00
Tampa Bay	0	0	0	.000	00	00
West						
Atlanta	0	0	0	.000	00	00
L.A. Rams	0	0	0	.000	00	00
New Orleans	0	0	0	.000	00	00
San Francisco	0	0	0	.000	00	00

Score table from the *Portsmouth*
(New Hampshire) *Herald*;
contributed by Gary Petersen

And it's hell on spelling, too.

Study: Long-term marijuana use harms mermory

From the Northhampton, Massachusetts, *Daily Hampshire Gazette*;
contributed by Jennifer L. Hoey

Newborn Babies Survive Murder Attempt by Distracted Editor!

Death Notices

GIRLS
• to Lee Ann and Colin Bell of Dowling, Monday, Jan. 5.
• to Leslie and Fred Stanford of Sudbury, Monday, Jan. 5.

• To Carol and David Fowler of Coniston, Saturday, Jan. 10.
BOYS
• to Jeanne and John Courtney of Sudbury, Sunday, Jan. 4.

• to Vivian and Bruce Greer of Sudbury, Tuesday, Jan. 6.
• to Cindy and Jim Meisenheimer of Sudbury, Tuesday, Jan. 6.

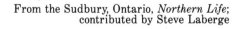

From the Sudbury, Ontario, *Northern Life*;
contributed by Steve Laberge

Ryan gets OK to kill religious school boards

SARAH SCOTT
THE GAZETTE

Education Minister Claude Ryan received legal backing from Quebec's highest court yesterday to abolish most Protestant and Catholic school boards and replace them with French and English boards.

From the *Montreal Gazette*; contributed by Bob Fiocco

From the Out of the Frying Pan Department

Steer Runs Away From Packing Plant, Enters Steak House

Associated Press

Omaha

A hulking Angus steer broke out of a cattle pen at a packing plant yesterday and crashed into the front doors of one of the city's best-known steak houses.

"He was excited and half-crazed, and I said to myself, 'I don't want that guy in here,'" said Tom Kawa, president and part-owner of Johnny's Cafe, who encountered the steer. "We would have had a hell of a rodeo."

From the *San Francisco Chronicle*; contributed by Dennis Senft

. . . and the deer can hardly wait.

Deer Hunters Balls are scheduled

There will be a number of Deer Hunters Balls on Friday in the area, including those at Pardners on Lake Buchanan, Hard Times on Hwy. 281 south of Marble Falls and at Ed's River palace on Hwy. 281 between Johnson City and Marble Falls.

At Parnders, the Deer Hunters Ball will run all night with 50-cent drinks for the ladies until 10 p.m. and "the best DJ in the Highland Lakes area!"

At Hard Times, the Deer Hunters Ball will run 8 p.m. until midnight with the band, "River City Rounders." There is a $3 cover charge. Call 825-3285 for reservations.

From the *Burnet* (Texas) *Bulletin*; contributed by Jamie Marmolejo

91

Lebanon will try bombing suspects

Coke Head To Speak Here

Humane society steps up pet destruction

Signs of Life, Part II: Let's Go for a Drive

Photo contributed by Michael Kiriazis

Photo contributed by Peter Brown

Just Do It

Photo contributed by
Mr. and Mrs. Jack A. Rye

Little Enigmas, Part II

Photo contributed by Regina K. Carter

Photo contributed by Lindsay Henderson

The Tooth Fairy Goes Corporate

Photo contributed by Edward Callary

From the Truth in Advertising Department, Part II

Some crack-ups are better than others.

Photo contributed by Lorraine Rowe

Photo contributed by Mike Straub

. . . and there's a penalty for early withdrawal.

Photo contributed by Kurt G. Hagdorn

OK, all you dead people, let's move it.

Photo contributed by Scott Mulligan

Banal byways

Photo contributed by Patricia Murdock

Photo contributed by Alan Barr

Photo contributed by Paul Cote

Just in case you're driving a 747.

Photo contributed by Joseph L. Gazza

That's odd—Rover was in the yard just a minute ago.

Photo contributed by
Joseph P. Oher

Where to Find the Nimblest Dink in the County

Photo contributed by Jim Muellerleile

Yeah, it's really somethin' to see, but the mist smells like ammonia.

Photo contributed by Jerry Labb

A Car with a Mission

Photo contributed by James Thomson

They'll slide right off your bumper.

Photo contributed by
Jim Motter

Okay, but remember: no touching.

Photo contributed by
David R. Selden

Honest, officer, I tried to sotp but I didn't know how.

Photo contributed by N. Leed

Just park and wait your turn, pal.

Photo contributed by Jim Wright

Only two blocks from Middle of the Road

Photo contributed by Dan Sevsek

Suicide's not the answer, especially if you have to take the shuttle bus.

Photo contributed by Dr. and Mrs. Wayne V. Miller

The Next Right

Photo contributed by Steve Stark

Photo contributed by Joyce Palmquist

Photo contributed by Kent Dundee

Emergency Instructions

Photo contributed by Cathy Lander

. . . then take your flasher and get out of here.

Photo contributed by Jerry Mauldin

Pull up to the pump and chow down.

Photo contributed by Niles Chandler

Photo contributed by Corey Moyerson

Wetter than those other brands!

Photo contributed by George A. Smith

Drive with care, caution, concern, concentration, and courage.

Photo contributed by Carl O. Kaufmann

. . . for it leaves tire tracks on the sunbathers.

Photo contributed by Linda Ontko Welp

Beware of purple rain.

Photo contributed by Larry S. Ferguson

. . . not on you, we hope.

Photo contributed by Floyd Gellerman

Bathing suits and Band-Aids required.

Photo contributed by Viki Bankey

Photo contributed by Jim Romano

Delivering Salvation

We grow 'em big, growly, and greasy.

We'd tell you what it is, but that would ruin the surprise.

Photo contributed by Allan A. Miller

Photo contributed
by R. B. Welch

Can't we just refer to them as being "physically challenged"?

Photo contributed by Al Dombrowski

Photo contributed
by Stephen P. Jones

Photo contributed by Michael Ritto

In fact, just stay away from my daughter altogether!

Photo contributed by Paul Smith

Photo contributed by Susan E. Henry

You live on the corner of *where*?

Photo contributed by Thomas Lines

Photo contributed by Susan Hoffman

Photo contributed by
Tom McCaffery

Just Buy It

Why don't you stay home tonight, honey—
I don't mind going to the garage by myself.

"FREE" *
We Do Head Jobs!

Aluminum head welding   Pressure testing
Camline repair and boring   Surfacing
Camshaft grinding and repair   Rocker arm grinding
*free deck warpage check
*free valve leakage check ($15.00 value)

SUPERIOR

HEAD 5 SERVICE

1-800-████████

FREYA and BROADWAY

From *Wheel Deals*; contributed by Boob Jackson

Who says we're not open-minded?

Photo contributed by L. Moskow

116

Dogs have gotten stupider since the sixties.

WANTED

DOG

Male Preferred

Must be of Collie strain and be
able to lip-read and be bilingual.

Apply:

BOX 9395,
CHRONICLE-HERALD

From a 1965 issue of the *Chronicle-Herald*;
contributed by Laura Robinson
and Mike Thompson

From the Well-Endowed Rabbit Department

From a craft supply catalog;
contributed by Art Mares

And next month, corned beef and cabbage pizza!

Photo contributed by Trevor J. Baker

Please Disregard the Zombies

From an unidentified Kansas newspaper; contributed by Gina Meyer

Nice Work If You Can Get It

From *The Columbus* (Ohio) *Dispatch*;
contributed by Gerald Kilbane

Just slap it on the counter and we'll see what we can do.

From the *Henrietta* (New York) *Shopper-Journal*;
contributed by Peter M. Gramiak

From the Friendly Greeting/Fond Farewell Department

Side-by-side ads in the *Glen Ellyn* (Illinois) *News*; contributed by Patrick J. Carmody

119

Sounds like the school needs a root canal.

It was drab, dark and dreary within the long halls of that old brick dental school in Downtown Baltimore, on the Autumn of 69! Built in the early part of the century, the institution resembled more of a Museum than a modern first rate facility, but being the first dental school in the world it maintained its scullery nobility within the confines of this decaying structure.

DAVID VINE D.D.S
Cosmetic & Reconstructive Dentistry   1010 - 71st STREET

Ad from the *Miami Beach Sun-Reporter*; contributed by Mary Jane Newborn

Please don't eat 'em in public.

A product label; contributed by Lorin Wegand

From the Who Wouldn't Department

Will swop tire ashtray collection for land in Maine, Vermont, or New Hampshire. M 731 NY

From Yankee Magazine;
contributed by Ken Brinnick

Take the A train.

PREGNANCY information. Free pregnancy tests. Confidential. On subway.

Ad from the Toronto Sun;
contributed by Debbie Czarnuch

No Charge for the Cadmium

Cadmium found in livers of lobsters from L.I. Sound

NEW LONDON (AP) — The state Department of Health Services is considering issuing a health advisory against eating the livers of lobsters taken from eastern Long Island Sound after samples of the green organs showed elevated levels of cadmium, a department official said Wednesday.

"We haven't issued an official advisory at this time, but when people call us up and ask us, we tell them they can reduce their exposure to PCBs and cadmium by not eating the hepatopancreas," said Bob Toal, chief of the department's toxic hazards section.

Side by side in the Meriden, Connecticut, Record-Journal;
contributed by Brian T. Lampher

Wanted: Warm Individual With Dressing

HI out there! I'm a young at heart lady, 49. Some things I enjoy are people, life, being honest & sincere, dining & dancing, quiet evenings, nature, laughing, family and friends movies, music, my job & some sports. If you are a man that enjoys similar things, I would like to eat you. So drop me a line to Herald Box CH1905.

From the *Calgary* (Alberta) *Herald*;
contributed by Mike Benton

He's a great catch, mom, except for one little flaw.

FORMER forester, vegetarian, 32 yr. old male, 3 degrees, seeking understanding and compassionate friend for occasional outings to all star wrestling. Reply to Box JP915 The Edmonton Journal.

From the *Edmonton* (Alberta) *Journal*;
contributed by Ryan Cromb

Dave the pet needs a pal.

PETS/LIVESTOCK

● *WHITE MALE, ATTRACTIVE*, 6'2", 38, fun loving, affectionate, many interests, desires to meet like female, 23-28 for friend. Write to: Dave, ██████████ (Send photo). (PE4-2)

From an unidentified California newspaper;
contributed by Mary Pyle

. . . and the summer will be a LuLu.

'Companions'

A cute male named Boo Boo seeks female named Woo Woo for a special summer.

Ad from an unidentified Canadian newspaper;
contributed by Jarett Sherman

Don't ask what it tastes like.

Product label from East Germany; contributed by Larry Kinner

Now! Assholes wherever you want them! Automatically!

Built-in Buttholer!

SAVE $40

Convertible free-arm sewing machine
Has 12 built-in, dial-to-sew stitches plus built-in button-
holer. Includes 4 utility, 4 stretch, 4 decorative stitches. Built-
in blind hemmer-mending stitch.

Ask about Maintenance Agreements

1560

Reg. $199.95

159⁹⁵

Sale ends April 1

From the *Kansas City Star*; contributed by Paul S. Imlay

123

Does Fido clash with your new decor?

From the *Carmel* (Indiana) *Highflyer*;
contributed by Mark E. Rogers

Third World English

Photo contributed by
Ronald R. Kyser

Bring your blemishes, and let's get down!

MEDICAL ASSISTANT/RE-CEPTIONIST Party time for dermatology practice. Drexel Hill location.

From the *Jerusalem Post*;
contributed by Beth Pfeffer

Watch out for the lady with the whip in the funhouse.

Amusement-park ride ticket;
contributed by Gary R. Winders

. . . and we'll gobble a while.

> If you were the lady in the Greyhound Grocery Friday, June 3:
> About 3:30, your 3-year-old was crying a little and my daughter was talking to her and said she was a little turkey like I was.
> **Call me at** ▮▮▮▮▮

Ad from the Jeffersonville, Indiana, *Evening News*;
contributed by Angela Carpenter

How many times have I told you not to let your body go off by itself?

Century 300 Car Seat

39⁹⁹
REG. 49.99

Has 5 point harness design and extra padding for safety and comfort.

From the *Providence* (Rhode Island) *Sunday Journal*;
contributed by Steve Browner

Keep the Windows Closed

PASS·N·WIND MOTEL

Pt. Salubrious, Chaumont, NY

NEW · MODERN
REASONABLE
6 UNITS
ELECTRIC HEAT · T.V.

From a promotional brochure;
contributed by Bill Woods

You might consider a face-lift, too.

Losing Hair???

Before   *After*

THE Drug-Free Alternative

(Distributorships Available)

From *New Life*;
contributed by Brian B. McColgan

That explains the powder burns on Blitzen.

The Gunsmith Shop
1147 N. Hwy. 67
Florissant, MO 63031

• Black Powder
  Supplies
• Gunsmithing
• Modern Guns
• Antique Firearms

EVEN SANTA SHOOTS BLACK POWDER

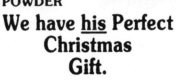

We have his Perfect Christmas Gift.

FREE LAY AWAY

Ad from an unidentified newspaper;
contributed by Jon L. Johnson

126

**Your kitchen's been strangled and your bedroom's been shot.
Trust me, ma'am, you don't want to go in there.**

Notice left in a Savannah, Georgia, apartment;
contributed by Larry D. Vincent

And it turned her life upside down.

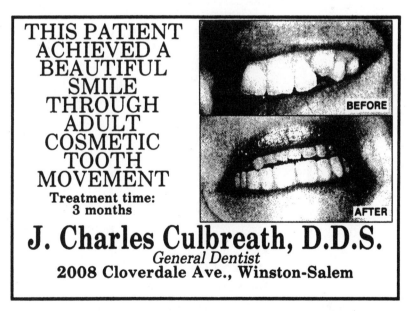

From the *Winston-Salem* (North Carolina) *Sentinel*;
contributed by Harold Johnson

Just follow those scratching guys.

Creighton University

Dept. of Dermatology
is looking for

volunteers with

JOCK ITCH

for a short study of a new
topical drug treatment

All treatment is provided *FREE* of charge

Confidential inquiries to:

Mon.-Fri. 8:00-4:30

From the *Omaha World-Herald*;
contributed by Ron Dufek

Been sitting on a toadstool?

**GENITAL WART
VOLUNTEERS
NEEDED**

FOR INVESTIGATIONAL RE-
SEARCH TRIAL USING INTERFER-
ON. TREATMENT AND LAB WORK
FREE. FOR MORE INFORMATION
CALL MONDAY-FRIDAY (9-4 pm)

NORTHERN VIRGINIA
BOARD CERTIFIED INFECTIOUS DISEASES

From the *Washington Post*;
contributed by Leigh Anna Ramstad

Big Sale at the Ook Store

**SALE
20% Off
All
Cookooks**

Coupons not valid on sale books
Good through 7-15-88

**Little Professor
Book Center**

Ahwatukee Mercado

From the *Ahwatukee* (Arizona) *News*;
contributed by Mary Riege Laner

Career of the Year

. . . and it doesn't hurt to be stupid, too.

From the *Kansas City Star*;
contributed by F. Dorsey Luchok

From the Vancouver, British Columbia, *Province*;
contributed by Caroline Vesely

From the Some Ingredients Are Better Left a Secret Department

From the Granby, Colorado, *Sky-Hi News*; contributed by Leo V. Piechocki

And you can live in the cinders when we're done.

From the *Fairbanks* (Alaska) *Daily News-Miner*; contributed by Robert Vigue

My old pair had me plugged up good.

From the Houston *Yellow Pages*; contributed by Terry Collins

And mazeltov to you, Mr. Wiggly!

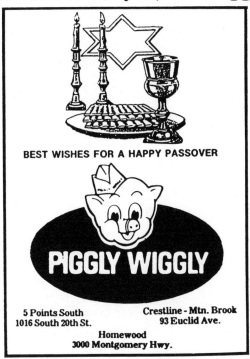

BEST WISHES FOR A HAPPY PASSOVER

PIGGLY WIGGLY

5 Points South
1016 South 20th St.

Crestline - Mtn. Brook
93 Euclid Ave.

Homewood
3000 Montgomery Hwy.

From an unidentified Alabama newspaper;
contributed by Katie Dye

A NATURAL CHOICE

"I'm happy! I've got gas!"
– Dave Hunter

From the *Vincennes* (Indiana) *Sun-Commercial*;
contributed by Judy Eaton

131

Gee, Dad's tastes just like that bottled junk.

From *Parenting* magazine;
contributed by Scott A. Edwards

Grandma's age-old recipe.

Photo contributed by Gail Heim

. . . from whence comes the saying "Dead as a dudu."

Photo contributed by R. B. Martin

Think small.

Coupon contributed by Joel Ryan Boline

Coming soon: Pavarotti Pantyhose.

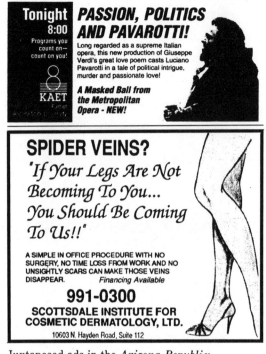

Juxtaposed ads in the *Arizona Republic*;
contributed by Wayne P. Barnard

Why's there a line down at Tyson's?

From the *Eureka Springs* (Arkansas) *Times-Echo*; contributed by Randy Freeman

Move over, Kaopectate.

Elixir from China;
contributed by Ophelia Chong

You're getting very sleepy, your honor . . . now repeat after me: "I find for the plaintiff . . ."

Coupon contributed by C. A. Woody

From the Instant Soup Department

Sales materials for a laboratory supply firm;
contributed by Graham Wren

Bird on a Hook

Business card contributed by John Smith

Mollusk Nerds

THE SMOKEHOUSE

Reg. $2.98 lb.

SMOKED OYSTER DINKS

$2.49 lb.

From the (Boise) *Idaho Statesman*;
contributed by M. Betournay

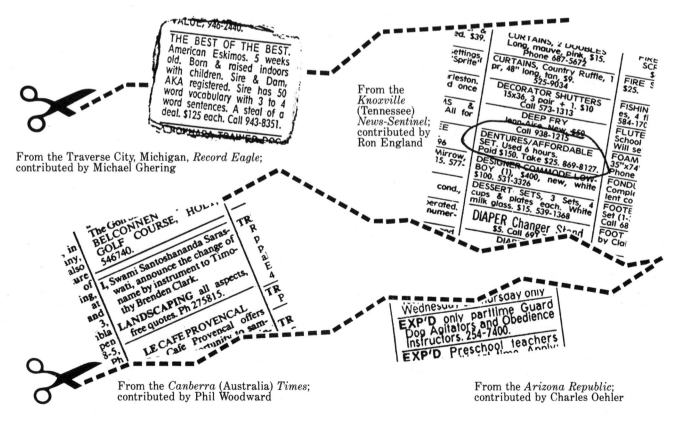

THE BEST OF THE BEST.
American Eskimos. 5 weeks
old. Born & raised indoors
with children. Sire & Dam,
AKA registered. Sire has 50
word vocabulary with 3 to 4
word sentences. A steal of a
deal. $125 each. Call 943-8351.

From the Traverse City, Michigan, *Record Eagle*;
contributed by Michael Ghering

From the
Knoxville
(Tennessee)
News-Sentinel;
contributed by
Ron England

DENTURES/AFFORDABLE
SET. Used 6 hours.
Paid $150. Take $25. 869-8127.

I, Swami Santoshananda Saras-
wati, announce the change of
name by instrument to Timothy Brenden Clark.

LANDSCAPING all aspects,
free quotes. Ph 275815.

From the *Canberra* (Australia) *Times*;
contributed by Phil Woodward

EXP'D only partlime Guard
Dog Agitators and Obedience
Instructors. 254-7400.

From the *Arizona Republic*;
contributed by Charles Oehler

137

Slogan or confession?

From the *Fairfax* (Virginia) *Connection*;
contributed by Charles Winkler

From the Hong Kong
South China Morning Post;
contributed by Kevin Fellman

Snacks and Semiautomatics

From *Consumers Press* of Montana;
contributed by Dave Farley

Love and Plagiarism

personal ads.
333-3662. FREE!

Scott, Just hearing your name, makes me smile, your beauty makes me short of breath, I pray that one day, you will say, I Love You, J.B. as much as I love you right now and I mean this with all my heart. I Love You, Baby. J.B.★★★P.S., I'm not going too fast, this is just me.

TERI, Just hearing your name makes me smile, your beauty makes me short of breath, I pray that one day you will say I Love You Scott as much as I love you right now. And I mean this w/all my heart. I Love You Baby, Scott.. P.S. I'm not going too fast, this is just me.

From the *Dallas Times-Herald*;
contributed by Paul Martin

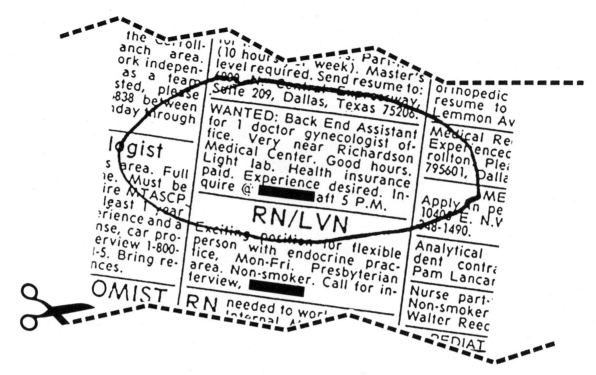

From the *Dallas Morning News*;
contributed by Larry Brautigam

The Last Honest Man

From the *Boston Globe*;
contributed by Michael C. Michalczyk

The astronauts complained it's clammy in there.

NOTICE
LAUNCHING OF SALAMA CONDOM

We wish to inform our esteemed invitees for the function of launching the

SALAMA CONDOM

scheduled for 12th June, 1991 at The Kilimanjaro Hotel, that it has been postponed due to an unavoidable circumstances.
We regret for any inconveniences that might have been caused.

90235/1559906

PHARMAPLAST (T) LIMITED.

From the *Daily News* of Dar Es Salaam, Tanzania; contributed by Chris Mawdsley

MISSING DOG HEAD

You finding Ling-Ling's head?
Someone come into yard, kill dog,
cut off head of dog.
Ling-Ling very good dog.
Very much want head return.
REWARD   Call ■■■■■

It's 6 a.m.
Do you know
where
Grandpa is?

Ad contributed by Dana Willey

Ha! And to think they all laughed at me in hand modeling school!

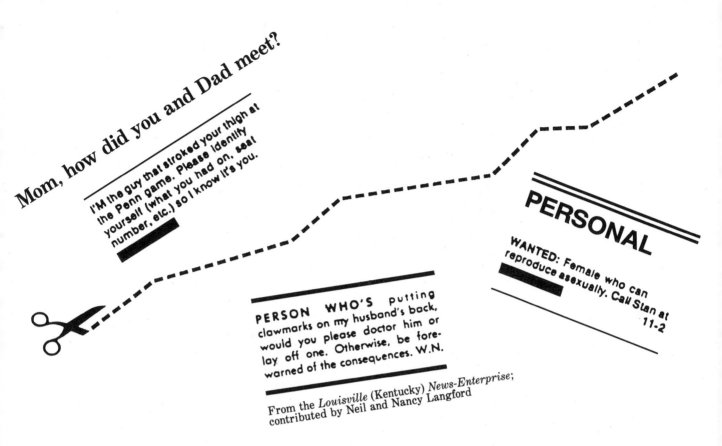

Mom, how did you and Dad meet?

I'M the guy that stroked your thigh at the Penn game. Please identify yourself (what you had on, seat number, etc.) so I know it's you.

PERSON WHO'S putting clawmarks on my husband's back, would you please doctor him or lay off one. Otherwise, be forewarned of the consequences. W.N.

PERSONAL

WANTED: Female who can reproduce asexually. Call Stan at 11-2

From the *Louisville* (Kentucky) *News-Enterprise*; contributed by Neil and Nancy Langford

We want to give you something to make your child vomit.

It's called Syrup of Ipecac. And every house should have some.

It's powerful medicine. A tablespoon will make your child vomit in less than 15 minutes. Not a pretty thought. But it's a lifesaver to the child who has accidentally swallowed poison.

This year, an estimated 500,000 children will be victims of accidental poisoning. Unfortunately, some of them will die.

Too many times this tragedy could be avoided if only there was Syrup of Ipecac in the medicine cabinet. Syrup of Ipecac can get the poison out –fast.

That's why Community Hospital wants to give you a free bottle. If you have a child under the age of 5, simply send us the coupon below. We'll send you a 1 oz. bottle of Syrup of Ipecac along with a brochure on what to do if your child or anyone in your family swallows poison.

At Community Hospital, we're always here when you need us. But, frankly, we want to do everything we can to see you never do.

Name
Street
City   State   Zip

COMMUNITY HOSPITAL OF ROANOKE VALLEY
Caring for Your Life and Lifestyle

National Poison Prevention Week
March 18-24

So, what was it like? Was Mary cute? What was Moses wearing?

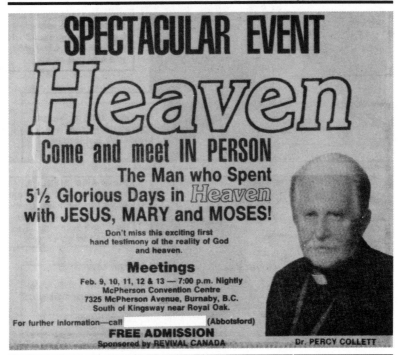

Ad from the (Vancouver, British Columbia) *Province*; contributed by Pat Bell

Specialized law.

I don't care how you stir up business, just do it!

Photo contributed by Luke Softich

Get involved with drugs before your children do.

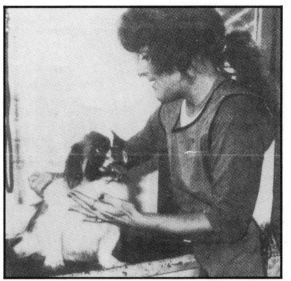

From the (Jefferson, Indiana) *Evening News*; contributed by Angela Carpenter

BRUCE, A FULL-BLOODED Pekinese dog, is looking good as Vicki Griffin grooms the pup at Pet Paradise. Both animals are for sale.

IMPORTANT
PLEASE READ YOUR AD
for errors the first day it appears. The Press-Enterprise Co. assumes no responsibility after the first insertion.
If you are placing an ad, correcting one or canceling one, PLEASE check your ad! All claims for adjustment must be made within 15 days after expiration of ad.

Contributed by Jon Fraser

Alone at last.

A PRIVATE WORLD - For you & your dong. See this cozy 1-2 bedroom home with its own fenced-dog run. In the 20's - and Owner wants it Sold Now!
SHERRY FRANKVILLE

146

The Amazing New
Pull-Off Cap

From the *Chicago Tribune*;
contributed by Steve Phillips

That's it, I'm getting rid of that hair ball once and for all!

From the *Arizona Daily Star*;
contributed by John M. Anderson

Sexual harassment
...it's everyone's
responsibility.

Ad published by the Administrative
and Clerical Officers' Association
of Sydney, Australia;
contributed by Ian James

acoa

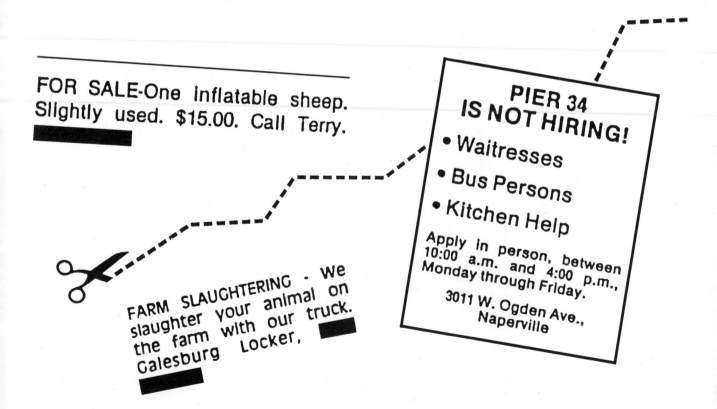

FOR SALE-One Inflatable sheep. Slightly used. $15.00. Call Terry.

FARM SLAUGHTERING - we slaughter your animal on the farm with our truck. Galesburg Locker,

PIER 34
IS NOT HIRING!

• Waitresses

• Bus Persons

• Kitchen Help

Apply in person, between 10:00 a.m. and 4:00 p.m., Monday through Friday.

3011 W. Ogden Ave., Naperville

DARKROOM TECHNIQUES

March/April 1983
Vol. 4, No. 2

$2.50

Developing Your First
Roll of B&W Film

Super Color Dupes From
Professional Equipment

Variable Contrast Advance
Ilford Multigrade II Paper

Senator Howard Baker's
Washington Photos

From a cover for the magazine
Darkroom Techniques;
contributed by James P. Schwartz, Jr.

OK, but first I want my mechanic to look at the tomatoes.

WANTED: 1967-72 muscle car; finished, unfinished, will trade dehydrated fruits, vegetables, macaroni, tomatoes, rice, flour, lemonade, 30 year shelf life. _____, MI.

It takes a big man to admit when he's wrong.

DEBBIE?

About that night I cracked up your new BMW over a concrete traffic barrier on Lake Shore Drive, I'm really sorry. What a horrible accident. When I crawled out the window you were still unconscious. I tried to pull you through, but your foot was stuck in the glove compartment. So I went to get help. I was less than fifty feet away when the gas tank exploded. Wow-Wee! Talk about explosions! I ran back and put out the fire with a wet beach blanket. THEN YOU WERE GONE! No Debbie! Where did you go? Are you okay? How's your foot? How's the car? Did they find your left arm? Look, I know you're probably a little upset. You have every right to be a little upset. I can understand that. But I don't think we should blow this thing up all out of proportion. In fact, I don't want to see anything else blow up for a long, long time. So, give me a call, or drop me a line. Let's be friends. Come over and we can play records and bang on my drums. Tell you Mom I said Hi.

Box 4499

Side-by-side ads from the *Honolulu Star-Bulletin*; contributed by Jerry Gauthier

You know, I remember when women weren't even allowed to vote.

Everyone knows the Hoboken Public School System is one of the worst in the State. Now, all the politicians promise reform. That's what we get, promises, promises, (not even Arpage).

FOR A NEW APPROACH VOTE
EVELYN ARROYO

Pd. by E. Arroyo Campaign

From the (New York) *Daily News*;
contributed by Dan Schwarcz

Born leader.

TERRY BARRY FOR CITY COUNCIL

"I'm schizophrenic and happy."

From the *Greensboro Daily News*; contributed by Teraesa Whitley

Heil Al Greenwood.

Honey, look what I found hidden under Junior's mattress.

Photo contributed by Darrell Garrison

Family fun.

OK, but those better be damn good references.

Talk about "Red Carpet Treatment"!

Part of an ad from the *Kansas City Star*;
contributed by James Mercer

Get it in writing.

"My husband and I have an understanding: He won't track dirt in my house while he's living and I won't pack 6 feet of it in his face when he's dead. I'm going to **Locust Hill Chapel Mausoleum** and get a pair of crypts while they're available and the price is low!"

Why don't you call ████████ also.

Stop . . . you're *both* right.

Photo contributed by Ron Gates

Attention Christian Hunters!

I am offering a special Bear Hunt to Christian Hunters. Come and share your faith in Christ with others on this special bear hunt. Devotions, prayers, and ex-changing Christian experiences are all part of this hunt.

For details call ▆▆▆▆▆ or Write: Christian Hunt, ▆▆▆▆
▆▆▆▆▆▆▆▆

From the *Denver Post*;
contributed by Lee Weingrad

Please Return My Blow-up Doll NO QUESTIONS ASKED Taken from Castle Creek Stage, May 30th. Her name is Amber. Call Ralph Dinosaur, ▆▆▆▆▆

From the (Grand Junction, Colorado) *Sentinel*; contributed by Douglas Cool

1173238. AM I A GOOD LOVER: The Answer Is In the Palm of Your Hand By Mark Shap & Alan Kahn. Look into your hand and discover the truth about your sexuality, your marriage, and your true emotional nature. Provides the decisive answers to such questions as: will I be deeply loved? St. Martin. Pub. at $4.95 / ONLY $4.45

Singer's Wanted: To sing at Conv. & Retirement homes. Good & Clean! nice body. Fully equipped to pull steer, good power, with claws. 100 couples! Pass it along. ▆▆▆▆▆

From an International House of Pancakes place mat; contributed by Joe Traynor

156

You've got one *sick* family, pal.

Photo contributed
by R. J. Swanson

Those fitness geeks will eat anything.

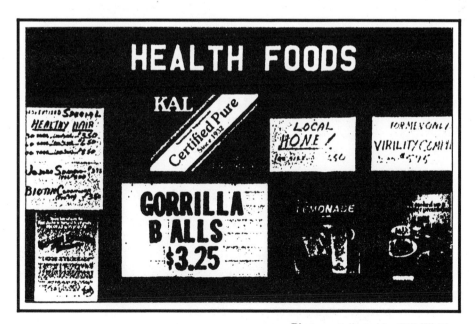

Photo contributed by Bill Whiting

Why, Jane, your cervical collar, it's . . . it's . . . gorgeous!

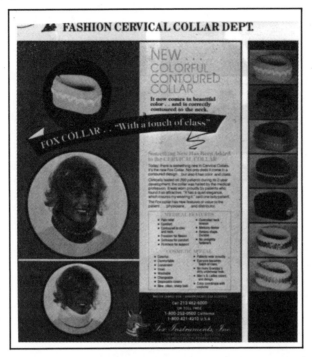

From a Fox Instruments, Inc., catalog

Contributed by Nancy Rimassa

Whatever happened to $2.00 a minute?

BUILDINGS - "ONE PHONE CALL CAN GIVE YOU a low cost erection." by direct telephone order from Ontario Manufacturer...28 x30 Value $3,700. Now $2,944. 40x50 Value $6,800. Now $5,593. Other sizes available 1-800-████████ Pioneer first in Steel Buildings since 1980.

From the (Canada) *News Advertiser*; contributed by Martin Roncetti

Coupon contributed by B. Hertz

Journey Into The Condom Future!

Join a federally funded study comparing a new space age condom with the best latex condom ... Free medical care/supplies to couples using condoms as birth control for 6 months ... **FOR INFORMATION CALL:**

Ad from an unidentified newspaper

Italian Cheese* Provolone Balls

1 44

½ Lb.
Reg. 3.98 Lb.

• Perfect for Snacks and Cooking
*In our Middletown Gourmet Shop only.

From the *Times* (Middletown, New York) *Herald-Record*;
contributed by Walter Ginelewicz

Hey Dad, when you pick
me up at school tomorrow,
can you take the Volvo instead?

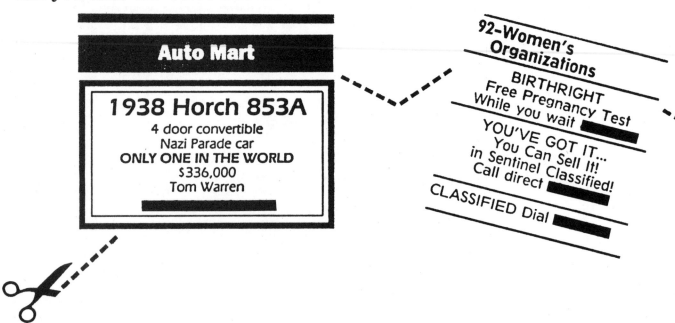

Auto Mart

1938 Horch 853A

4 door convertible
Nazi Parade car
ONLY ONE IN THE WORLD
$336,000
Tom Warren

92-Women's Organizations

BIRTHRIGHT
Free Pregnancy Test
While you wait

YOU'VE GOT IT...
You Can Sell It!
in Sentinel Classified!
Call direct

CLASSIFIED Dial

Signs of Life, Part III: It's Showtime!

Photo contributed by Thomas Powell

Photo contributed by Gail Williams

Loud, Libidinous Videos

Photo contributed by
Warren Couvillon, Jr.

Hi-ho, Loni!

7:30 **5** **Evening** Take a test ride in the
newest ride in Disneyland; Loni Anderson.
8:00 **4** **Movie** ★★ *The Impostor* (1984)
Anthony Geary, Lorna Patterson. A con
artist charms his way into the principal's
post at a Midwestern high school and

From the *Seattle Post-Intelligencer*;
contributed by Jeff Swanson

OK, who snuck the guy in here?

From the Pittsburgh edition of
TV Guide;
contributed by Lou Pappa

If you want a decent IQ, it's a buck and a half.

Photo contributed by Gerry Evans

Bring earplugs.

From the *Charleston* (South Carolina) *News & Courier*;
contributed by J. Tatum

I never did trust those Fly Gods.

The worse it is, the more they like it in Philly.

. . . and it goes in the potty.

CHANNEL 4

6.0 THE CHANNEL FOUR DAILY.
9.25 THE ART OF LANDSCAPE.
11.0 AS IT HAPPENS, at London Zoo.
12.0 THE PARLIAMENT PROGRAMME.
12.30 BUSINESS DAILY, with Susannah Simons.
1.0 SESAME STREET: The letters are S and H and the number is 2.
2.0 POWERBASE (T) (rpt.).
2.30 THE MEASURE OF SUCCESS: Saving.

From an unidentified European newspaper;
contributed by James Little

Cancellation. "God's Trying to Tell You Something," scheduled for 8 tonight in the Civic Center has been canceled. Tickets can be returned to the Civic Center box office or to the place of purchase for a refund.

From the *Des Moines Register*; contributed by Kara L. Gipson

The Shadow At Bay

Photo contributed
by Mark Mattison

7 5 20 Legmen Jack falls for a college student who is also a part-time hooker in trouble with a white-slavery ring operator intent on killing her. 1 hr.

9.10 Superman (Rpt) (G)
9.30 Woody Woodpecker: 21 Billion Dollar Boner (Rpt) (G)

23 MOVIE ★½ "Helter Skelter" (1949, Comedy) Carol Marsh, David Tomlinson. A detective gets involved with a wealthy socialite who can't seem to stop hiccuping. (2 hrs.)

11 Dick Van Dyke Rob, under the influence of science fiction, fears that a walnut will steal his imagination and his thumbs.

50 Movie: "Lady Liberty" Sophia Loren. An Italian woman on her way to a wedding—attempts to go through customs with a large sausage (1972) ★★

12 Star Trek Mr. Spoc) blows his cool and almost gets Capt. Kirk killed when an overwhelming mating urge takes possession of him. (To 3:30)

12:00 **2 Vega$** Dan frantically searches for a large quantity of cocaine. (R)

8 12 Just Kidding Topics children discuss include why cows don't wear pants. and what to do with a shotgun at the dinner table. (Repeat)

(CMX) Movie ★ "The Beas Within" (1982) Ronny Cox, Bib Besch. A woman is raped on her honeymoon by a hairy-legged creature. 'R'

24 CBN 700 Club Abortion facts; the NFL's greatest bloopers.

7 MOVIE ★TENTACLES (Thriller, 1977). What has eight legs, no nose an eats people? Shelley Winters. (1 hr. 50 min.)

168

I Do, You Do, We Do Do

I do, I do, but don't stand too close, okay?

Long-Cox

Shannon Marie Cox and Mark Edward Long were married Aug. 30, 1989, at Graceland Wedding Chapel, Las Vegas, Nev.

The bride is the daughter of Dale Cox Jr. of North Aurora and the late Pamela Cox. The groom is the son of Janet Grady of Punta Gorda, Fla., and John Long of Aurora.

The bride is a 1988 graduate of West Aurora High School. She is employed by Farmers Insurance Group. The groom is a 1982 graduate of East Aurora High School. He is employed by Berry Bearing Co.

They live in Aurora.

Mr. and Mrs. Long

From the Aurora, Illinois, *Beacon-News*; contributed by Jack Schultz

I do, I do, but I have here a list of fifteen card-carrying Communists in this very wedding!

Joseph-McCarthy

Michelle Carolyn Joseph of Sierra Madre and Sean Robert McCarthy of Pasadena are planning a June wedding. She is the daughter of Mrs. Carrie Joseph of Sierra Madre, and the granddaughter of Mr. and Mrs. William Mann of Whittier. McCarthy is the son of Mr. and Mrs. Dennis McCarthy of Pasadena.

The prospective bride attended Westridge School in Pasadena, and is now a senior studying speech pathology at Cal State Northridge. Her fiance attended La Salle High School in Pasadena and received a degree in English from UCLA. He teaches social studies and

MICHELLE JOSEPH and SEAN McCARTHY

English as a Second Language in the Los Angeles Unified School District.

From the Pasadena, California, *Star News*; contributed by Travis Kelly

170

I do, I do, but shouldn't we have boots and an umbrella?

Storm-Flood

Mr. and Mrs. Wallace Storm of Birmingham have announced the engagement of their daughter Pamela to William Flood, son of Donald Flood of Novi and Barbara Flood of Naples, Fla.

The bride-elect is a graduate of Andover High School and is employed as a marketing coordinator at the Thomas A. Duke Co.

Her fiance is a graduate of Farmington High School and is employed as a complex supervisor for Village Green Management Co. Both attended Ferris State University.

A late March wedding is planned at the First United Methodist Chuch of Birmingham.

From an unidentified Michigan newspaper; contributed by Alan Valentine

I do, I do, but I should hope so, big fella.

Ball-You

Sophia You, daughter of Mr. and Mrs. Yong Su You of Seoul, South Korea, and Maj. Randall N. Ball, son of Mr. and Mrs. Billy C. Ball of St. Albans, were married May 12 at the Yongsan Military Installation in Seoul.

From the
Charleston (West Virginia) *Gazette*;
contributed by Joe Freeman

I do, I do, but please, don't let go.

Cox-Held

Married June 10 at St. Joseph's Catholic Church were Angie M. Cox, Marion, and Rick H. Held, Orlando, Fla. The Rev. John McDermott performed the 2 p.m. ceremony. A reception for 200 guests followed at Longbranch Supper Club.

From the *Cedar Rapids* (Iowa) *Gazette*;
contributed by Bill Irwin

I do, I do, but did we have to get married at the ballpark?

Beers, Franks

Lewis Beers of King of Prussia, Pa., and Mrs. Richard Foust of Roland Park in Baltimore have announced the engagement of their daughter, Elizabeth Skeath Beers, to Thomas Stone Franks, son of Mr. and Mrs. Robert Franks of Annapolis.

A graduate of West Chester University, Miss Beers is the director of athletics at Oldfields School in Glencoe.

Mr. Franks, a graduate of St. Mary's College, is corporate computer training coordinator for Provar in Towson.

A spring wedding is planned.

**ELIZABETH S. BEERS
and THOMAS S. FRANKS**

From the *Washington Post*; contributed by Chris Nugent

I do, I do, but couldn't we have potatoes for a change?

Brown-Rice

Ormond Beach Memorial Gardens was the setting June 3 for the wedding of Patricia Ann Rice and Michael Scott Brown, with the Rev. Frederick Frustch officiating.

From the *Daytona Beach* (Florida) *News Journal*; contributed by Gary Demianycs

I do, I do, but then I'd say we were made for each other, wouldn't you?

Kuntz-Dick

Lisa Renee Kuntz and Gary Wayne Dick plan to be married in a 12:30 p.m. ceremony July 14 at Carmel United Methodist Church in Carmel, Ind.

From the *Evansville* (Indiana) *Press*; contributed by Gavito Solis

I do, I do, but keep your hands to yourself 'til after the reception.

BUNN-GRABS

KING — Ashley Elizabeth Grabs of King and Kevin Brett Bunn of Raleigh were married Saturday at King Moravian Church.

The bride is the daughter of Mr. and Mrs. Omnie Omily Grabs Jr. of King. Parents of the bridegroom are Mr. and Mrs. Franklin Bunn of Raleigh.

Bunn

After a reception at King Recreation Acres, the couple left on their wedding trip to Florida. They will live in Raleigh.

From the Raleigh, North Carolina, *News and Observer*; contributed by Mike Sellers

I do, I do, but good garter belts are hard to find.

Stock -King

The marriage of Miss Gail Elaine King and Mr. Frederick Joseph Stock III was solemnized Sept. 2 at St. Louis Cathedral. The bride is a daughter of Mr. and Mrs. Franklin Theodore King and the bridegroom is a son of the late Mr. Stock Jr. and the late Mrs. Jenny Marie Avella Stock. The Rev. Ray Wilhelm, O.M.I., officiated at the ceremony, which was followed by a reception at the Windsor Court Hotel.

From the *New Orleans Times-Picayune*; contributed by Bonnie LeBlanc

I do, I do, I *must* say!

Martin-Short

Lisa Rae Short, daughter of Mr. and Mrs. Raymond C. Short of Perry Hall, and Stephen Andrew Martin, son of Mr. and Mrs. Joseph A. Martin of Kingsville, were married Oct. 15 in the Loyola College Chapel.

Stephanie Short and Joseph Martin Jr. were honor attendants.

Both Mr. and Mrs. Martin are graduates of Loyola College. She is a master's candidate at the University of Baltimore. He is a CPA with Wooden & Benson.

Mrs. Stephen Martin

From the *Baltimore Sun*;
contributed by Nancy Thayer

I do, I do, but someone just stole our Yugo.

Good-Loser

Mary Ellen Good of Hummelstown, daughter of Mr. and Mrs. Thomas T. Good of Sutton Avenue, Hopwood, became the bride of Stephen T. Loser, son of Mr. and Mrs. Thomas J. Loser of Hershey on July 1 at St. Joan of Arc Church in Hershey.

The Rev. John Hoke officiated at the service.

Given in marriage by her father, the bride wore a full length blush satin brocade gown with ballgown neckline and sleeves, basque waistline and chapel length train. A veil of illusion fell from a satin headpiece of roses and pearls.

MR., MRS. LOSER

From the *Uniontown* (Pennsylvania) *Herald-Standard*;
contributed by Mike Skoda

I do, I do, but who are all those short guys?

Snow-White

Immaculate Conception Catholic Church provided the setting Feb. 10 for the wedding of Anne Elizabeth Snow and Danny Lee White, both of Cedar Rapids. The 2 p.m. ceremony was performed by the Rev. Phillip Schmitt.

From the *Cedar Rapids* (Iowa) *Gazette*; contributed by Janet Gagne

I do, I do, but who's gonna walk Dino?

FLINT-STONE

CAMBRIDGE — Mr. and Mrs. Wayne S. Flint of Cambridge and Mr. and Mrs. Carl Lewis of New Britain, Conn., announce the engagement of their daughter, Bonnie Lynn,  of Barre to Timmy Carol Stone, the son of Mr. and Mrs. William Stone of Barre and the late Karlene H. Stone. The bride-to-be is a 1985 graduate of Montpelier High School. She is employed as a customer service representative at the Granite Bank. Her fiance attended Spaulding High School. He is a mechanic at Stone's Service Station. A May 19, 1990, wedding is planned.

From the *Rutland* (Vermont) *Herald*; contributed by Derek Yesman

Miss Brenda Sue Powers

Local man engaged

From the *Worthington* (Ohio) *News*; contributed by Alan Brady

175

Two Feet and Digging

Frost-Line

Jeri-Lyn Frost and Donald Wayne Line, both of Indianapolis, were married March 9 in Bethany Lutheran Church.

Their parents are Mr. and Mrs. Gerald W. Frost, Mrs. Gary T. Leathers and Verle D. Line, all of Indianapolis. The couple graduated from Indiana University. The bride is a member of Alpha Chi Omega. She is a registered nurse in pediatric intensive care at Riley Hospital for Children. Her husband is a member of Chi Phi. He is owner of Beverage Enterprises Inc.

From the *Indianapolis Star*;
contributed by Lucille Parr

Fowler-Colon

Susan Michelle Fowler of Odessa and Gregory Lawrence Colon of El Paso were married April 20 at Odessa Tabernacle Church with the Rev. Sam Jordon officiating.

The bride is the daughter of Mr. and Mrs. Johnny E. Fowler of Odessa. She is a 1983 graduate of Permian High School and a 1988 graduate of Texas Tech University with a degree in marketing. She is employed by Roadway Express in El Paso.

The groom is the son of Mr. and Mrs. Willard Linebert of Louisville, Ky., and the late Malcolm Colon. He is a 1983 graduate of Lewisville High School in Lewisville, a 1987 graduate of the University of Texas at Austin with a degree in finance and is a 1991 graduate of Texas Tech School of Medicine in Lubbock.

**Mr. and Mrs.
Gregory Lawrence Colon**

From the *Odessa* (Texas) *American*;
contributed by Michael L. Schuff

... and slaw on the side.

MRS. MUSTARD
. . . Allison Pickels

Mustard-Pickels

Allison Leilani Pickels and Charles Stoll Mustard Jr., both of Athens, Ga., were married March 24.

From *The* (Columbia, South Carolina) *State*; contributed by John W. Barrett

Tamara Long

Long-Moose

HERTFORD, N.C. — Miss Tamara Kay Moose and Mr. Dwayne Andrew Long exchanged vows Saturday, April 8, at 2 p.m. in Holiday Island Park.

From the Virginia Beach *Virginia Pilot/Ledger Star*; contributed by Wendy Woodruff

Conjugal cramp

Sharpe-Payne

Savanna Lynn Payne and Robert Franklin Sharpe III were married July 6 at North Park Presbyterian Church.

The bride is the daughter of Paul R. Payne of Corpus Christi and LaRue Westbrook of Lewisville. The bridegroom is the son of Mr. and Mrs. Robert Franklin Sharpe Jr.

Honor attendants were the bride's mother and the bridegroom's brother, John Kenneth Sharpe of Boulder, Colo.

The couple will live in Austin.

Sharpe

From the *Dallas Morning News*;
contributed by Sue McMorris

. . . and a dandelion bouquet, please.

Engagements

Weed, Pickens

Former Fremont resident Mary Kathleen Weed and Samuel David Pickens announced their engagement on Jan. 5 at the home of the bridegroom-elect's parents in Barre, Mass.

They plan to wed on March 20 at the Sisters of the Holy Family Chapel in Mission San Jose. The bride-elect is the daughter of retired U.S. Air Force Lt. Col. and Mrs. Hampton Francis Weed of Fremont. She graduated from Moreau High School in Hayward, the University of California, Davis, and received a Ph.D. from the Sorbonne in Paris. She works for Hewlett-Packard in Geneva, Switzerland.

The bridegroom-elect is the son of Dr. and Mrs. Samuel Claude Pickens of Barre, Mass.

He is a guaduate of Quabbin High School in Barre and Boston University.

He is Editor-in-Chief of "Contact," for Nakia Consumer Electronics in Geneva.

From the *San Francisco Examiner*;
contributed by Dana Hernandez

Johnson - Wax

Vows of marriage will be spoken on April 20, 1991, by Michelle Lee Johnson and David John Wax, both of Creek Drive, Kentwood.

The bride-to-be is the daughter of Sue Johnson of Lake Odessa and Gerald Johnson of Hastings.

From the *Hastings* (Michigan) *Reminder*;
contributed by Kim Eldred

Beaver—Trimmer

Mr. and Mrs. Gary Trimmer

NEW OXFORD — St. Paul's "The Pines" Lutheran Church was the setting for the Dec. 15 wedding of Janet L. Beaver and Gary R. Trimmer. The Rev. B. Tim Wagner performed the double ring ceremony at 5 p.m.

A resident of 303 N. Bolton St., the bride is the daughter of Charles and Ann Beaver, Northumberland RD1. The bridegroom is the son of Edwin and Romaine Trimmer, 2147 Hunterstown/Hampton Road, New Chester.

Given in marriage by her father, the bride wore a pale pink wedding gown of satin. It was styled with a natural waistline, and the satin bodice featured a shirred center panel of re-embroidered lace with sequins and pearl drops. The long, satin sleeves had a double shoulder puff which extended into a fitted sleeve of English net and satin. The back bodice featured a deep V and a butterfly satin bow at the waistline.

The full satin skirt was edged at the hemline with a a scalloped border of re-embroidered lace. The skirt extended into a sweeping cathedral-length train.

Lisa Tomalavage of Dauphin was the matron of honor. Chosen as the bridesmaids were Melissa Frantz and Sandy Kase, both of No.thumberland. Brittany Beaver of Northumberland was the flower girl.

Serving as the best man was Willie Musselman of York Springs. The ushers were Jeff Murren and Charles Becker, both of Hanover. Jason Trimmer of Abbottstown and Dustin Beaver of Northumberland were the ring bearers.

Ruth Dellinger of Gettysburg provided the organ music. The vocalists were Marcia Knorr of Hanover and Ted Schott of East Berlin.

A reception for 175 guests followed in Heidlersburg Firehall. The newlyweds are living at 489 Frazer Road, Aspers.

The bride is a 1980 graduate of Shikellamy High School and a 1987 graduate of Bloomsburg University. She is pursuing a master's degree at Western Maryland College and is a teacher for Lincoln Intermediate Unit No. 12.

The bridegroom is a 1983 graduate of New Oxford High School and is a carpenter and crew leader for Barry Bechtel General Contractor Inc.

From the Sunbury, Pennsylvania, *Daily Item*;
contributed by T. C. Retallack

Paul — Newman

Jill Ann Newman, daughter of Dr. William and Judie Richman of Hollywood, FL and Rodger and Adele Newman of Akron, OH, has become engaged to Steven G. Paul, D.V.M., son of Norman and Florrie Paul of Boca Raton.

From the *Miami Herald*; contributed by David Rutman

Roberts-Pinkstaff

Cheryl F. Pinkstaff and Arthur L. Roberts Jr. were married March 9 at Los Altos Methodist Church.

The bride is the daughter of Robert A. Akins Sr., Louisville, Ky., and Sadie M. Moles, Hurricane, W.Va. A graduate of Milpitas High School and San Jose State University, she is a police officer in Newark.

The bridegroom is the son of Arthur L. Roberts Sr. and Ruth A. Roberts, Mountain View.

From the *San Jose Mercury News*; contributed by Kevin Cronin

Ruth Ellen Herring

Barefoot, Herring Engaged

Ms. Toshiko Higo Herring of Spring Lake announces the engagement of her daughter, Ruth Ellen Herring of Linden, to Eldridge Rudolph Barefoot Jr. of Spring Lake, son of Eldridge Rudolph Barefoot Sr. of Spring Lake.

The wedding will be held on May 4 at Bethel Baptist Church.

From the *Spring Lake* (New Jersey) *News*; contributed by Glenn Riccio

And now for the best-groomed couple . . .

DIANE and DENNIS HAYRE

Yong Photography

Hayre-Combs

Diane Amy Combs and Dennis Duraine Hayre chose the First Presbyterian Church as the setting for their May 11 wedding.

From the *Stockton* (California) *Record*;
contributed by Pat Jones

Sack the minister.

engaged

Lawrence - Taylor

KERHONKSON — Mrs. Vena Quick announces the engagement of her daughter, Chesty Stacia Lawrence, to Tracy Michael Taylor, son of Mr. and Mrs. Victor M. Taylor, Rosendale. Miss Lawrence is also the daughter of the late Edward William Lawrence.

The future bride is a graduate of Kingston High School and BOCES. She is employed at Mohonk Mountain House, New Paltz.

Her fiance attended Rondout Valley High School. He is a self-employed carpenter.

A wedding in June is planned.

From the Middletown, New York, *Times Herald Record*;
contributed by Richard Roda

Overtime Nuptials

LONG-DAY

Lisa Denise Day and Douglas Anthony Long were married April 6 at Rivercliff Lutheran Church in Roswell.

The bride is the daughter of Priscilla Edwards of Lexington, S.C., and Dr. Richard R. Day of Rome, Ga. She is a graduate of the University of Georgia and is employed by E.T. Booth Middle School.

The bridegroom is the son of Lucretia Davies of Savannah and Thomas E. Long Jr. of Green Cove Springs, Fla. He is a graduate of Virginia Commonwealth University and is employed by Dean Rusk Middle School in Canton.

After a cruise to the Caribbean, the couple will live in Woodstock.

From *The Atlanta Journal-Constitution*; contributed by Chuck Buell

. . . and a bib for Lobo, please.

Wolfe-Spittle

Barbara Ann Wolfe of Oak View and John Spittle of Ventura are announcing their engagement and plan to be married on June 1 at the First Christian Church in Ventura.

The bride-to-be, daughter of Bernie and Shirley Wolfe of Oak View, is a 1986 graduate of Ventura High School. She is an order clerk for Paradise Chevrolet.

The prospective groom, son of Bob and Gloria Spittle of Ventura, is a 1984 graduate of Ventura High School. He is an auto mechanic for Paradise Chevrolet.

From the *Ventura County* (California) *Star Free Press*; contributed by Tom McDonnell

A.k.a. Frankfurter

LONG/HAMBURGER

Julie A. Long and Michael J. Hamburger were joined in marriage Sept. 9 at Congregation Neveh Shalom. The bridegroom wore his father's ring for the ceremony. Maui, Hawaii, was their honeymoon destination.

The bride, a self-employed hairdresser, is the daughter of Gena K. Long of Forest Grove. The bridegroom, a national sales manager, is graduate of the University of Oregon. Inga Hamburger of Lake Oswego is his mother.

From *The Oregonian*; contributed by Richard H. Kingsley

Sand 'er down and she'll be just as good as new.

Fuller-Bumps

CHINA — Heidi Jo Bumps and Dean Edward Fuller were married Oct. 13 at the Baptist Church. A reception followed at the Winslow VFW. The bride is the daughter of Arulde and Christa Bumps. The bridegroom is the son of Guy and Ruth Fuller of Palermo.

The maid of honor was Wendy Nelson of Albion. Bridesmaids were Gloria Keay, Noel Martin and Susie Nelson, all of Albion, and Tiffany Bona of Waterville.

The best man was Jerry Fuller of Palermo. Ushers were Daryl Keay, Ricky Nelson and Rusty Nelson, all of Albion, and Trevy Bumps.

The bride, a graduate of Erskine Academy, is employed by LaVerdiere's Super Drug Stores' main office. Her husband, also a graduate of Erskine Academy, is employed by R&D Masonry.

The couple resides in Albion.

Mr. and Mrs. Dean E. Fuller
(Heidi Jo Bumps)

From the (Waterville) *Central Maine Morning Sentinel*; contributed by R. E. Nelson

Thank God, now I can finally get rid of the embarassing name "Cockman."

Cockman-Dickman

Dr. and Mrs. Donald Dickman

Carrie Anne Cockman, formerly of Davenport, and Dr. Donald G. Dickman, Cheyenne, Wyo., were married May 29 at St. John's Church, Creighton University, Omaha, Neb.

Their attendants were Maureen Maley, Maureen Mullin, Julie Stockert, Peggy Dickman, Pam Dickman, Kari Greguska, Troy Peterson, John Sammis, Ben Lass, Chris Cockman and Joe Cockman.

Their parents are Len and Lory Cockman, Newton, Iowa; and Charles and Shirley Dickman, Cheyenne.

Street - Lay

Mr. and Mrs. Dean Street of Toledo are pleased to announce the engagement of their daughter, Diane Lynn, to Lonnie T. Lay, son of Mr. and Mrs. Arzo Lay of Toledo.
A March 27, 1993 wedding is planned.

Love-Organ

SHERWOOD — Mary Theresa Organ and Robert Sterling Love were married Saturday in Immaculate Conception Catholic Church by the Rev. John O'Donnell. Parents are Mr. and Mrs. Thomas P. Organ and Mr. and Mrs. Robert E. Love, all of Sherwood.

Honor attendants were Lori Howard and Victor Cummings. The couple will reside in North Little Rock.

From the Arkansas Gazette; contributed by Jack Finch

MRS. ROBERT LOVE

Swallows, Wright

Kim Raquel Swallows and Robert Craig Wright exchanged wedding vows in a 2 p.m. ceremony on July 30 at the Eastside Kirtland Air Force Base Chapel.

The bride is the daughter of Kathleen M. Swallows of Honolulu. The groom's parents are Mr. and Mrs. Keith Wright of Northville, Mich.

Gina Swallows and Deidre Montaño, sisters of the bride, were attendants. Keith Wright, the groom's father, was best man.

The couple spent their honeymoon in Telluride, Colo. and Durango, Colo.

They are making their home in Rio Rancho, where the bride is a homemaker and the groom is a technical sergeant of Life Support serving in the United States Air Force.

Mrs. Wright

Signs of Life, Part IV: Eat and Get Out

Where to Find the Best-Fed Trucks in America

Photo contributed by Billy Cox

Not at the table, please.

FATHER'S DAY

at the

Oyster Reef

**SPECIAL! Prime Rib or Filet Steak
& Cajun Prawns . . . PLUS Complimentary
Glass of Champagne and a "Hooker"
for Dad!**
Casual Dining Over The Water - 11:30 am to 10 pm

10th Avenue & EMBARCADERO OAKLAND

From the *Oakland* (California) *Tribune*; contributed by Bill Hoch

We boiled 'em, and now they're mad.

Photo contributed by Michael P. Morgan

Restaurant or rest stop?

Notice: Seating Limited When Chef Excited

Photo contributed by Craig MacFarland

Photo contributed by William Stage

Notice: Please Pay in Advance

Photo contributed by Margaret von Biesen

No shoes, no shirt, no cummerbund, no service.

Heavy on the studs, hold the spats!

Photo contributed by Chris Gutscher

Photo contributed by Richard Terrill

Come Be the Main Course

Hey, can you guys do "Feelings"?

Aberrant Burgers

Photo contributed by Clark Kidd

Photo contributed by George Smith

Photo contributed by Ron Mayers

Just don't expect Giancarlo Giannini.

Photo contributed by Guy Major

Here's your hat; what's your hurry?

Photo contributed by Carl G. Jacobson

Why Kids Shouldn't Read

Photo contributed by Herm Albright

Separate Seating or Catch Your Own?

Photo contributed by Bob Ring and Lynn Ruby

Yum.

Photo contributed by Timothy Harnett

Anonymous photo contribution

Photo contributed by Judi Rogers

Because you said you were tired of McDonald's, that's why.

Photo contributed by G. D. Young

. . . and a side order of Lysol, please.

Photo contributed by Rory Peterson

Swim and Party with Your Supper

Photo contributed by Gerry Beaney

You Should See 'Em Dance

Photo contributed by J. Rowley

Do you have any idea how hard it is to kill one of those things?

Photo contributed by Mike Ruplinger

Remember to duck when she turns around.

Photo contributed by Lou Carlson

Featuring light snacks from hell's kitchen

Photo contributed by Don M. Miller

Home of the Well-Done Burger

From a West German newspaper; contributed by Eric Damm

Sighting Number 187,308

Photo contributed by Lynn Wiegard

Humpty's pissed off. Get your own.

Photo contributed by Wayne Leonard

Photo contributed by Fran Guyott, Jr.

Photo contributed by Leo Buccellato

. . . and don't stop for gas either.

Photo contributed by Paul Ellis

It sounds like war in there at lunchtime.

Photo contributed by Ron Ramsden

. . . He was over at Belchers making noise.

Photo contributed by Angus Bromley

Please unwrap cabbage before eating.

Photo contributed by Jeremy Foster

Beans and a Great Big Exhaust Fan

Photo contributed by Josh and Matt Levine

Pour me another prime rib, Al.

Photo contributed by Marci Ward

Seafood Malaise

Photo contributed by Christopher M. Landrum

Photo contributed by Christopher M. Landrum

Fun for People Who Spit When They Talk

Photo contributed by Wendy Viets

... featuring the famous three-foot sausage!

大旺飯
BIG WONG RESTAURANT

Photo contributed by Edward G. Kosco

After sushi burgers, dessert.

Photo contributed by Lori and Bob Butler

Photo contributed by Louis Angelwolf

Photo contributed by Jay Goldstein

"Hey honey, what did you say your nickname was back in college?"

Photo contributed by Bobbie Scannell

Photo contributed by Allston James

Photo contributed by Brian Grady

Photo contributed by Tom Hahn

Photo contributed by Ray Check

Front and back of a pack of matches; contributed by Rodd Zolkos

Tales from the Crypt

From the Do Unto Others as Was Done Unto You Department

Photo contributed by Greg Blair

. . . but not quick enough.

Look, I got here as soon as I could.

Photo contributed by Randy Palmer

Photo contributed by Lee Taplinger

The Old Hot Dog Burial Ground

Photo contributed by John F. Ybarbo

Wrap 'Em Tight And Send 'Em Parcel Post

Ad from *The Baptist Record*; contributed by Walter H. McDonald

Frankly, Kent, from the condition of the bodies, it must have been Superman.

Photo contributed by John J. Frongillo

R.I.P., a Great Bandstand American

Photo contributed by Brad Irons

... and we'll always remember you for your, well, you know.

Photo contributed
by Christopher Clyde

... but not for long.

Photo contributed
by Herm Albright

Don't worry, boss, I buried it where no one will ever guess.

Photo contributed by Herm Albright

You just can't keep a *bon homme* down.

Photo contributed by Paul Sutherland

Last Stop for Roger Rabbit

Photo contributed by
Zach Thompson

Some guys just won't let it go.

Photo contributed by Scott Wingerson

Headstones for Dead Phonies

Photo contributed by Leon D. Ver Schure

Funeral Menu

MARY PIZZA

Mary Pizza of Hudson died Sunday at her sister's home in Greenport.

She was born in Italy.

Survivors include her husband, Harry Pizza of Hudson; three sons, Anthony of Binghamton,

HOWARD TOPPING

Howard J. Topping, 73, of Wynantskill, father of Jonnie Davis of North Chatham and Pamela L. Topping of Valatie, died Monday at St. Peter's Hospital, Albany.

Born in Troy, he lived there and

Side-by-side obituaries in the *Independent*; contributed by R. Kane

Photo contributed by Al Theis

Tickles would have wanted it this way.

Photo contributed by Russ Meyer

Photo contributed by George Mickelson

Let's see, I have twenty minutes before I'm due back at the office, what to do . . . what to do . . .

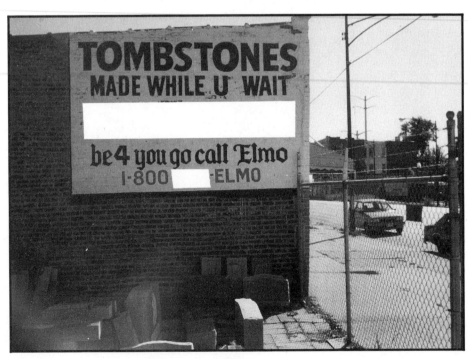

Photo contributed by Steve Keating

It sounds so beautiful when you put it that way.

A CEMETERY WHERE PETS
CAN ROMP AND PLAY
IN THEIR METAL BOXES
DOWN THROUGH THE
AGES OF ETERNITY

Crummy
Funeral Homes

Photo contributed by John Smallwood

Stop laughing, you insensitive bastards!

In memory of Steve "Mike" Detmer who was killed by a bowling ball on January 4, 1985.

We will never forget you.

June Detmer,
Ann Detmer &
Ernie Detmer

Signs of Life,
Part V:
Risky Business

Photo contributed by Steve Jones

Photo contributed by Robert J. Wiersewa II

Who Named the Business?

Photo contributed by John Mayer

Photo contributed by Josh Williams

Fresh! From Chernobyl Dairies, it's . . .

You can't wear them, but take our word for it: they're really clean.

Photo contributed by Ranger Bob

Photo contributed by Greg Gattuso

Shoot the Piano Player

Photo contributed by
Daniel K. Purlsey

Lighting from Hell

Photo contributed by
Daniel C. McHugh

Car Dealers Without Pants

Photo contributed by Jerry T. Wilson

Photo contributed by David E. Holubitsky

I'd say about $54 million, not including the bleachers.

Photo contributed
by Steve Thomas

I'll take a dozen, uppercase please.

Photo contributed by Tom and Beth Gould

I know you're busy, Lord, but could you please clean my rug?

Photo contributed by Ron Chase

See the Lady in Net Stockings for Details

Photo contributed by Douglas A. Danke

. . . a division of Thank You, Ma'am, Inc.

Photo contributed by Vint Davis

. . . for Sexy Mouse and Duck Wear

Photo contributed by Shaun Ivory

From the guys who brought you cement boots . . .

Do you take 'em away, or do I have to bring 'em over?

Your prices are good. Your store is great. In fact, there's only one thing I'd change, Mr. Dumfart.

Photo contributed by Dale Fundling

We forget about the hard part, and pass the savings on to you!

Photo contributed by Linda Peterson

Don't call us, we'll call you, unless the damned thing doesn't work again, in which case you'd better call us after all.

Photo contributed by Richard Carter

Watch out for the tongue prints on the wash.

Photo contributed by Danny Wallace

If you're looking for commitment, try the hardware store.

Photo contributed by Bert Prestridge

Dancing Derrières

Photo contributed by
Gale Gardner

Burgeoning Business

Photo contributed by
B. L. LaCoyne

Sure, just after I paid full price.

Photo contributed by Mark Coulston

Employment for the Frustrated

Photos contributed by Thomas J. Ferri

When it absolutely, positively has to get there . . .

Photo contributed by Robert Stevenson

. . . with the most convincing sales force north of the border.

Photo contributed by Greg Swanson

A bucket of killies or some dame in fishnet stockings?

Photo contributed
by Greg Lawrence

. . . Featuring the Famous Gesundheit Coffee Shop

Photo contributed
by Mary Campbell

So a weimaraner ate your poodle? You want to make something of it?

Gimme a mermaid and caption it "Woof."

Photo contributed by David R. Hiller

Photo contributed by Lance K. Trask

Go ahead. Squeeze an udder. Kick a hoof. She's as good as new.

Photo contributed by Mark R. Youtzy

Don't miss the big swizzle stick sale.

Photo contributed by Gord Kurbis

Mr. Cox and Mr. Cox are tied up, but Mr. Cox will see you.

Photo contributed by Michael Paston

New, Used, and Rebuilt

Photo contributed by Richard Carter

Photo contributed by Rick Kneidel

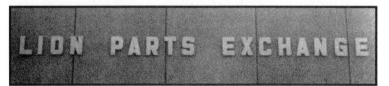

Photo contributed by S. Veres

Please bring your own anesthetic.

Photo contributed by David Jolles

A John by Any Other Name

Photo contributed by
Michael Johnson

Photo contributed by
Gary Tillotson

Photo contributed by Louisa Beal

Keep It Clean

Photo contributed by Jon Krassenstein

Well, almost anyway.

Photo contributed by Keith Benkery

If you like the movie, you'll love the industry.

Photo contributed by Robert Stanek

Colossal Sales

Photo contributed by Jim Mantel

Photo contributed by Phil Steffen

Photo contributed by Jack Marshall

. . . and heaven is a quieter place.

Photo contributed
by R. E. Miller II

Bring your own potato chips.

Photo contributed by
Michael Frank

Hunting's More Fun When You're Plowed

Photo contributed by
Will Veber

Earphones for minnows

Photo contributed by Jim Kavalier

Fish Rubs

Photo contributed by Joan C. Serivani

Home of the Jiggle Shows

Photo contributed by Mary Nell Drust

No smoking, please. Our last dog disappeared when someone lit up.

Photo contributed by Kimberly Montoya

Kuntry Kousins

Photo contributed by David Marshall

Photos contributed by David Marshall

Photo contributed by Paul Egan

They hate the hair dryer.

Photo contributed by Hans Tischer, Jr.

Photo contributed by Deb Jonaitis

Sorry. We don't carry it.

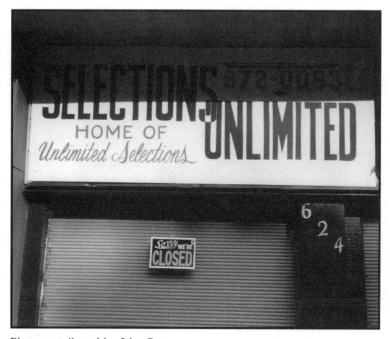

Photo contributed by John Goese

Complain and they cry.

Don't worry, you won't feel a thing.

Photo contributed by Gina Meyer

Photo contributed by Stephen D. Miller

Photo contributed by Dixon Bowles

Photo contributed by Don Liverani

The Pride of the Swiss

Photo contributed by Ivor Jones

MISSI G, Part II

Photo contributed by Brian Carter

Photo contributed by Stacy Fisher

Photo contributed by Beth Kuebler

Photo contributed by Jack Kunces

It'sa costa lessa uppa the road.

Photo contributed by Scott Morris

Photo contributed by Paul Nine

You better get over here, boss. The washers attacked the freezers, and there's Freon all over the place.

Photo contributed by Christina Renke

For Light Sleepers

Photo contributed by Marc Brewer

Look but don't squeeze.

Photo contributed by Daniel Barth

Rest Rooms for Customers Only

From a Filipino calendar;
contributed by Roland Hanewald

Shades of Justice

Photo contributed by Mark Barra

Mystery Motor Lodge

Photo contributed by E. A. Minahan

Shoppers' Choice: Brand-Name Motels

Photo contributed by Joe Patrick

Photo contributed by Richard Terrill

Photo contributed by Scott Pritchett

Photo contributed by Rita Whale

Photo contributed by Andrea McGuire

We're practically giving them away!

Photo contributed by David Edwards

No, dear, I don't think a cat fancier's parking lot would be full of four-by-fours, pickups, and semis.

Photo contributed by Carl Salas

A present for the ex?

Photo contributed by Dan Felter

. . . and a wedge of Muenster to hang over the fireplace.

Photo contributed by David Deeds

Toward Greater Consumer Confidence

Photo from unidentified magazine; contributed by Sean Swidnicki

Photo contributed by David W. Wilhelm

Photo contributed by David Kovl

So where is . . . THE MERCHANDISE?

Photo contributed by Peter Lorenz

Wrinkled minnows and bible-pressed worms.

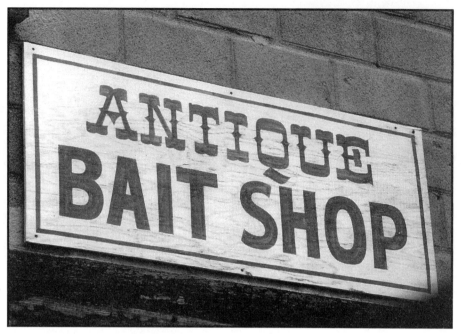

Photo contributed by Ed Thornburg

. . . where the ambulance squad drowned doing mouth-to-mouth.

Photo contributed by Randy Bender

Captivating container or passionate pugilism?

Photo contributed by David Thrower

Where all medical options are exhausted.

Photo contributed by Steve Makela

Photo contributed by Rick Kestenbaum

When you want the job done right . . .

Photo contributed by James Stinson

Try Our Famous Chico Chops

Photo contributed by Jerry Kehn

The Good Book and a Can of Lysol

Photo contributed by Paddy O'Leary

. . . and Pat takes in laundry.

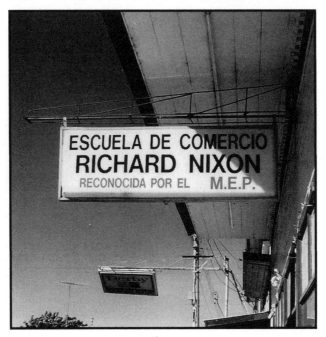

Photo contributed by Steven M. Krauzer

Wildlife Washers

Photo contributed by Bonni Backe

Photo contributed by Ken Koshiol

Photo contributed by Christopher A. Foster

We'll troubleshoot your bison.

Photo contributed by Edward G. Kosco

重生漢醫院
OWH'S ACUPUNCTURE
TEL· 460-4026

Photo contributed by Ray Sanow

Hi, I'm interested in buying a house . . . *OUCH!*

DICK PINCH
REALTY
56410

Photo contributed by Bill Stuehler

Photo contributed by F. H. Martin

Get your sheets their whitest.

Photo contributed by Ron Coles

Photo contributed by Phillip Kuhlenbeck

It's the happiest place on earth!

Photo contributed by M. M. Winnett

Hey, some of these guys don't even have cars.

Photo contributed by Casey Batule

Photo contributed by Bill Edie

Photo contributed by M. M. Winnett

Photo contributed by M. M. Winnett

Uh oh, Spot's chasing those invisible cats from Venus again.

Photo contributed by Jim Auiles

Photo contributed by T. A. McDermid

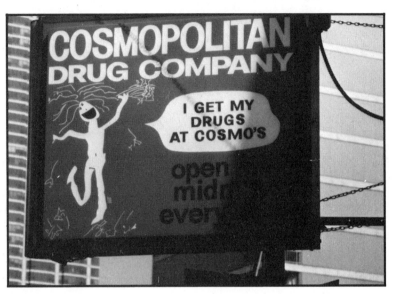

Photo contributed by Brian Galford

Photo contributed by Laurence Faith

One-stop shopping.

Can you make me look like Keith Richards?

Put on your prettiest evening gown, dear, we're going dancing!

Photo contributed by Pedar Ness

A doctor who truly empathizes with his patients.

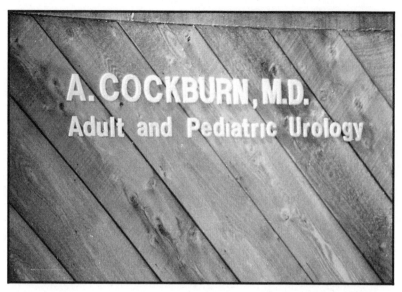

Photo contributed by Mark A. Barroso

Photo contributed by Jeffrey Cohen